T0171656

TRANSFORMATION–

The Alchemy of Grace

Carol Simons

BALBOA.
PRESS

A DIVISION OF HAY HOUSE

Balboa Press books may be ordered through booksellers or by contacting:

Balboa Press
A Division of Hay House
1663 Liberty Drive
Bloomington, IN 47403
www.balboapress.com.au
1-(877) 407-4847

ISBN: 978-1-4525-0369-1 (sc)
ISBN: 978-1-4525-0370-7 (hc)
ISBN: 978-1-4525-0368-4 (e)

Library of Congress Control Number: 2011963462

Because of the dynamic nature of the Internet, any web addresses or links contained in this book may have changed since publication and may no longer be valid. The views expressed in this work are solely those of the author and do not necessarily reflect the views of the publisher, and the publisher hereby disclaims any responsibility for them.

The author of this book does not dispense medical advice or prescribe the use of any technique as a form of treatment for physical, emotional, or medical problems without the advice of a physician, either directly or indirectly. The intent of the author is only to offer information of a general nature to help you in your quest for emotional and spiritual well-being. In the event you use any of the information in this book for yourself, which is your constitutional right, the author and the publisher assume no responsibility for your actions.

Any people depicted in stock imagery provided by Thinkstock are models, and such images are being used for illustrative purposes only. Certain stock imagery © Thinkstock.

Printed in the United States of America

Balboa Press rev. date: 01/17/2012

Contents

Introduction

It is I, the voice of all consciousness, which is vibrating in unison and as one with you. You will recognise me because I am the voice you hear in the stillness of your soul. What you read in this book is personal to you, for in a way you wrote it from the truth that is your true being. As you read these words, you will sense they are an echo, for within you lies the same truth. Rejoice as your soul affirms its own words, timeless words of wisdom that are so familiar. These words have always been within you. As you remove the cloak of fears and falseness in which you have shrouded yourself, you allow yourself to sing in oneness with all that is.

Relax into your being, put away any limitations of your mind, and open yourself to your soul. The truth of your beingness is yours to behold, and as you do, you will be transformed by the alchemy of grace.

I need many voices to proclaim the same message—the message of love and oneness. Yet even more than voices, I need channels open to the promptings of spirit, through which I am made manifest to those who remain in darkness. Through you, I reach those who seem dead in spirit. Those beings respond to divine love, as this is the catalyst to awaken their souls, for although their souls never really sleep, they are denied by darkened minds. The message of love is one that says, "Arise and awaken to the light that has lain dormant within you throughout many lifetimes." Within each and every living entity there are already stirrings as the spirit prepares to accept the truth. This realization of a new way of being in itself is enough to shake the earth, but by knowing truth, all fear is vanished as love is manifested on earth.

Transformation: The Alchemy of Grace

Beginning and ending reside in infinity.

I AM infinity; in me, you are.

We dwell beyond beginning and ending; we dwell in eternity.

CHAPTER 1

The Consciousness Of Energy

Let Us Begin

Let us begin. In the beginning was the word. This word was made available to every man, woman, and child. This word was *grace*. It is by grace that you live; it is to grace that you owe your very existence. It is grace that calls you back to herself. I, your maker, the creator of all, call you through grace. I formed you. In my mind I formed you, and I loved you before you took the form you are now in. I love you now.

It is my presence that stirs within you as you admire a beautiful sunset. This is the part of me that resides in you—the part of yourself that you deny. Can you feel that inner stirring as I admire my own handiwork? The awe that you feel—that indescribable joy that you feel at times when you are overcome with the emotion of joy—these are times when you recognise the creation as something of sheer beauty, yet you do not recognise me.

I dwell within you. I am residing within your very spirit—within your life force. Can you feel the love within your blood as it flows through your veins? I am in every cell of your being. I am within your DNA. There is much to look at in the world around you, but it is limited. Look within, beyond limit. The me you find within is infinite. We never end, you and me. We are connected and interwoven; we exist for all eternity. In me all your joys are made full. Beyond time and beyond space, I am the Alpha and Omega, the beginning and the end. You began in me, and you return to me, the source of all. In this way I am the beginning and the end, but truly, as I say unto you, there is no end and no beginning to me. I have always been and will always be, for I am the eternal presence. Nothing exists anywhere in your universe and beyond, except me. I am the All.

The Energy Of All

I am divine consciousness, the energy of all. All that exists is energy, my conscious energy, for I am conscious of all that is. I am conscious of both what is formed and what is not formed.

You are parts of my consciousness within a form. All knowledge and truth of your being lies within you.

Your soul is your consciousness; it is your individual part of me. If you know your soul, you know me.

Your body is the vehicle your soul chose to experience this life with. Your body is the perfect match for *all* the lessons and experiences your soul wanted for this journey.

Your mind is a receptacle for the knowledge gained by your unique experiences.

I created you as parts of me, and yet you are individuals. I am within you, and you are within me. In that way, you are within each other. I exist in all things and in the absence of things. I *am* in all.

Beyond Defining

I exist in the silence. I exist in the vastness you constantly try to cover with images, smells, or sounds—anything to feed the hunger of your senses. *It is only because of an incessant need for a point of reference that you try to define me.*

I *am*. I *am* beyond defining.

I cannot be confined, yet I am not beyond experiencing. When you touch my silence and know me, there are no questions, only awareness of infinity, and even beyond awareness I *am*. Where I *am*, there is no need for questions, no need for answers, for I *am* the all of all. I *am* the highest of the high.

I *am* beyond definition and beyond naming. Nothing in your limited reality can define me. It is only when your reality becomes one with mine, when your consciousness becomes one with mine, that you know me beyond defining.

You know me beyond defining in that place where you are beyond defining.

I *am* with you always.

I *am* with you through all your trials and through all your joys. I *am* with you always. I *am* within you. In every experience you have and every hardship you endure, I *am* with you. I never leave you, yet I do not force my presence upon you. You have free will.

You can choose whether to accept me or deny me. It does not even matter if you do not believe in me. It does not even matter if you consider yourself unworthy; my love for you is constant.

I Love You Always

I love you. My love is all encompassing. Whether you accept me or not, I *am* with you always. My breath is the very air you breathe; my essence is in every cell of your body. I loved you before you took form. I love you always; regardless of the form you are in or not in.

You were formed by love, and to love you return.

Within my love, you find your existence. Your existence is an expression of my love. Thereby, knowing your very essence, your soul, and your existence, you know my love. I am love; therefore, you know me.

My love is energy so great that it may not be seen, but the effects of my love are visibly evident. My love for you is a zealous love, encompassing all.

Find yourself, and know your true self. I am the love you find. Know yourself as love. Know me.

Satisfaction

Many of you perceive yourselves to be individual beings disconnected to the rest of the world. You believe that you are born and you die, and this lifetime is for you to achieve your goals. These goals are to prove to the world that you are worth something. You also pursue them for your own satisfaction. These achievements may help to make you feel successful in your attempt to show something for your time on earth. Those of you who appear to have successfully achieved your goals spend the rest of your lives in fear of losing them. You are driven to fill the thirst for satisfaction by any means you can, be it in materialism, children, food, alcohol, drugs, or other props promising to fill that void. You may even do countless acts of good works, helping others, believing this is your contribution to the world and in that way finding a sense of satisfaction in your life, yet you are all starving your own souls. You are always wondering what you can do next. You strive for completeness instead of just being satisfied and fulfilled in the knowledge of yourself.

You can never be completely fulfilled until you see through the illusion of separateness and recognise that you are eternal entities, joined in spirit to all.

You are a part of me. You pervade my very essence, and I yours. *You* are my love. You are not a little, separate being; you are a part of the oneness of all. You are a part of me, and I am a part of you. You are a part of everyone else, and they are a part of you. Together we are one. Whether you believe it or not, it is a truth, and in your innermost being, you know that to be so. For within your innermost being is your soul, and your soul knows you as a spiritual being. The spiritual being that you are is eternal, omniscient, and divine. Your spiritual self knows no separation, only unity with the all. Your spiritual self is one with all. *You are limitless.*

You Are Limitless

Light and love make up your very being. Listen with your ears, and look with your eyes. To your own self be true, and awaken to who you are. The happiness you seek is within. The freedom you seek is within. The satisfaction and completeness you seek are within. Rejoice in finding fulfilment within, and rejoice in the peace that it brings. Rejoice in me.

Stand in me, in your own divinity, and claim your place within me. Your spirit already knows this place. Your spirit calls this place home.

You cannot earn the keys to the kingdom. These are given in grace to the seeker. Put your soul first before all else. Finding and knowing your soul allows your life to flow according to spirit.

Know Yourself

You have always felt that there was more to life, that something was missing. The awareness of your true self is what is missing. By acknowledging who you are and walking in the way of oneness, you are finally fulfilled and finally home. This is your purpose. This is what you seek. Find yourself, know yourself, and *then* you know me. Look within. I am within you. Your true being is my home. I dwell in each of you, in all of you. You are all a part of me.

You are my beloved. I care for you. Commune with me.

CHAPTER 2

The Peace In Knowing Your True Self

Know First Yourself, Know Me

Question Yourself

Secure In Your Being

Life's Game

Treasure

I Will Lead You

I Am Calling You

Know First Yourself, Know Me

Knowing yourself is the first step to freedom—freedom from the need to be right, freedom from the need for materialism and power, freedom from the opinions of others, freedom from negativity, freedom from discontentment, and freedom from illusion. You can know yourself by looking within, finding your truth, and witnessing your old nature as it works to keep you in the darkness through its fear.

Become aware of yourself. Notice your reactions to others and situations. Begin to respond through light rather than react through ego.

Your old nature, reacting from fear, becomes exposed; your new nature, responding from light, becomes your being.

Wake up to yourself. Witness your old nature reacting from fear and trying to protect itself. Your true nature needs no protection. Your true nature cannot be destroyed, for it is invincible.

You who have studied and sought and believe in the oneness of all but do not yet feel in every fibre of your being that you are in *all* of creation, you are only a breath away from doing so. You may think you are enlightened, and you may see others as yourself most of the time, but when you know the fullness of our unity as it sweeps over and through you, all doubt is gone. You are a part of all creation, even the lowliest of insects and the fiercest beasts. You are a part of it, and you *know* it.

Know yourself in me; claim the divinity that is yours.

Question Yourself

Know yourself so intimately. Know the reason behind all the emotions you feel, and understand the meaning of these reasons as they relate to you. It is in this way that you question your very being and get to your core. When your core beliefs are exposed, you can then go beyond those beliefs to a place of silence, emptiness, and soul. It is then that you know the truth of your being.

When you know the truth of your existence, I *am* revealed to you.

When you recognise yourself in me and me in you, only then can you be bold in your divinity. You are in everything as I *am*. You are in the skies, the mountains, the birds, and all others. You are in me, and I *am* in all.

Secure In Your Being

Finding your soul wakes you up to your true self. Your true, omniscient self is both free and secure. Having that inner peace and love means you are in harmony with the kingdom within. There is no longer need for external success to validate your existence. You no longer want because you are fully satisfied. You are secure in who you are. You do not need the approval of others, nor do you feel threatened by any criticism. You know your truth, and that is very powerful. You feel safe in the oneness of the universe. The love you feel is reflected in your joy.

It is my love, your love, our love, one love.

Through my grace, you are transformed from one who is lost and looking to find oneself to one who is found, knowing the essence of *no self.* Your true self cannot be contained in identity; your true self is limitless, powerful, and love.

Your true self is an awareness of me; your true self is awareness of all.

Life's Game

This life is but an illusion. Think of it as a dream and wake up. You have been asleep long enough. It started as a game to subjectively feel creation and its different experiences without remembering that within me you actually created it. You agreed to hide within a body that is ruled by a mind, and the objective of this game was to get the body and mind to find their missing part by looking within. You knew that by looking within, they would discover truth, which would mean that their existence would be then exposed as part of the illusion.

Treasure

Do not be attached to feelings of power, approval, or capitalistic gain. These are empty substitutes for the peace you find within your soul. Seeking happiness, peace, and freedom outside of yourself is fruitless. It is only in fear and desperation that you search for these beyond yourself.

The treasure you seek is within, hidden in plain sight.

The treasure within is yours forever. You can never lose it, and it cannot be stolen from you. It is eternal. You find the material things and egotistical indulgences that you once valued appear shallow in comparison to your internal treasure.

Awake! Awake and become the light of love, peace, happiness, and satisfaction to the others who still grasp outside of themselves.

This is your purpose. Find yourself, and then help others to end their search.

I Will Lead You

Follow me. Follow me, and I will lead you to green pastures. You will not go back to the darkness but forward, gathering more light. Even the valleys that once held darkness for you are now bathed in light. Through your soul, I will lead you to places you do not yet know. Trust me.

Trust me, for within me you dwell, sharing the kingdom of oneness.

Follow the voice of your soul; follow me.

Wisdom and grace flow through you as you become that clear channel of truth and love. Wisdom and love reflect outward from your inner being to those who are floundering, still looking for happiness. You are a beacon of light to those who are not even sure of what they seek, knowing only a void within themselves that cannot be filled. Trust me; follow me.

I Am Calling You

For those of you still feeling as if you are in the darkness, fearful for your own survival, insecure, and trying to protect your self-image, know that the light is real. Become aware of your soul.

Your perceived self-image is the illusion.

The truth that is *you* has no need for security, for it survives eternally. I am calling you to wholeness through your soul. Listen within your emptiness. Many of you are afraid to look into your own darkness, into your own void. Don't you see that by choosing not to look within, you deny yourself the very existence you have been looking for?

I reside within your soul; your soul resides within me. I call to you through your soul. Attend to my call for your completeness. I love you. Heed the call of your soul. Rest in love. I *am* calling you.

CHAPTER 3

The Purpose Of Living

My Love

My love for you is beyond measure. It is beyond your understanding. You understand love on the human level, but love in the fullness of me is many hundreds of times more. You cannot even begin to understand. I am energy, a consciousness, but I am love. You cannot imagine a love greater than any energy you have ever experienced, greater than the energy from your sun, which was also created for you. You cannot possibly know the depth of infinite love at this time, but you will ultimately know that love because that is what you are. When all the illusions have faded into the nothingness they are, there is only love, but not love as you know it; it is pure, unadulterated love. Every hair on your head is counted. Every blade of grass and every delicate feather are all formed from this love. Love considers every minute detail, each intricate pattern of a butterfly's wing, the distinctly different tastes of each herb, and your unique voice.

There Is No Randomness in My Creation

Everything is ordered in perfection, all interrelated, and all part of my ultimate oneness. Each piece has its unique place. This intermeshing of all life on earth correlates to your essential presence above. As above, so below. The fact that many of you still view yourselves as separate beings does not alter the unity of my reality.

Your beliefs may be wrong, but my truth does not need belief to be true.

You may be bound in your thinking by your false beliefs, but my truth sets you free.

Your soul is part of me. It is easier to look within to find your soul than to look outward to find me, and in so doing, you will come to know yourself. Thereby you will know me. I *am* the all in which you exist. In me you live, breathe, and have your being. Know yourself—know me. I formed you, and my spirit lives within you.

I love and adore you, my beautiful creation. You are mine and I am yours, forever held in love.

Reaching Others

There are some who, recognising our union, ask if I can use them to reach others. Within you is access to the divine will for your life. As you allow it to unfold, you reach the others you are meant to reach. People come and go in your life. Some come to help you with a life lesson, others come to receive from you, and others just come to be with your being. Be more aware of those around you. Be more awake to your soul's promptings, and in all instances, act from compassion. Just as feeding the roots of a tree feeds its many branches and leaves, honouring your soul enables you to know the right action or inaction to take to compassionately enable others (human and otherwise) on their journey.

Comparisons

Do not compare your value to another. See everyone as your equal, for you are all equal, all one. There is nobody more valuable than you, and there is nobody less valuable than you.

You are all unique. Each of you has your own sacred path.

Each of you is beyond a value that can be measured. You are impossible to value. You are worth more than all the earth's gems, for you are priceless. There is nothing to feel jealous over. The only things of true value are the eternal things. All else will pass away. It is senseless to feel jealousy over a mirage, as that is all it is. It is senseless to feel jealousy over another's soul because you are all one. It is senseless to feel jealous at all.

Remembering

Your existence in me is absolute because I am everything, but you chose to experience life as a sole entity, being only you, separate from all others, including me. In order to experience this separateness, you needed to forget that you were one with me. Each of you came from truth—that being why when you hear a truth it resonates in your being and your cells' vibration. It manifests in feeling, and it is then that the truth goes from believing to knowing. You know within every cell of your body that the truth is real.

YOUR DNA CONTAINS A MESSAGE

The truth is linked to me. In each one of you, your DNA is coded to respond to truth. In that way, the truth will set you free. The DNA within your cells contains a message to yourself; it is the blueprint, the code to help you remember your greatness. When we agreed to this experience, we agreed to put a safety net in place. This is the peace you discover when you find the truth held within your soul. It is the peace that indicates you have safely arrived. It is my peace within your being. It is peace that flows throughout your being as you come into the realisation that you have found what you were searching for. When you land on the safety net of peace, you know your search is over.

Any time you feel the pain of separation or the lack of peace, look within and find me within yourself, remembering then who you are.

The cycle of lives only exists for you until you choose to release yourself from that guise of separateness and return back to your omniscient self. That is the reason you chose your lifespan—to pass the tasks you set yourself, knowing that you could take one or more lifetimes to do this. After passing the set tasks, you would move up a level, so to speak, and be faced with a new challenge, a new task.

Your purpose is to rediscover yourself and reveal yourself in your divinity.

The Final Task

In the process of your own learning, if you reached the highest level, your task was to help others know who they really were. By remembering themselves, they then have that option of coming back onto that endless merry-go-round of living and dying or returning home. You who know me, the God within yourself, or know yourself to be as me, know the importance of this final task, for it is part of yourself that is missing. The missing parts themselves do not know they are missing; they have eluded themselves. I liken it to the man who is downing but cannot see the lifeline in front of his face. These other souls are drowning in separateness. Throw them a lifeline, and let them swim in the sea of memories as they return to me. Give them the choice, which is ultimately theirs, but so many do not realise that. They have eluded themselves for too long. They desire the game to be over, but they have forgotten how to go out.

Show them the way home. Teach them my truths, and remind them of the nature their being, their soul. When you show them who they are, they will remember me. By taking grace, using grace, and being grace, you will help them come home.

CHAPTER 4

The Truth Of Judgement

Forgiveness

There may be those in your life who you feel have wronged you. Do not be swept up in believing the roles they are playing in your life. See through the great illusion. They are but spirit. They are the same as you in spirit. The wrong they did to you was nothing but a part of their script. Learn the lesson they brought to you, for if you refuse to, you will learn your chosen lesson another way. It was you who chose to learn such a lesson as part of your life experience.

By becoming aware of your own inner truth, you transcend the need for forgiveness because there is nothing to forgive.

There is no heart too hard for my love to soften.

Look inward, know yourself, and discover the truths within, and by grace, the absorption of this knowledge sets you free.

Your soul guides you once you take your first step; its light draws you closer. Unforgiveness is among the negative emotions that ego takes advantage of to keep you closed to the openness and truth of spirit.

Unforgiveness is the tie that keeps you bound to the one you are condemning. Loosen the tie and let others go, releasing yourself to freedom.

Judgment Of Others

There are two types of judgment: the judgment of a being in terms of race and physical and mental capacity (these are judgments based on what cannot be changed easily, if at all) and judgments of behaviour of that being. To judge a soul in the first way is damaging to your own being because he or she is one with you, and you are my children. To judge behaviour, use discernment. Recognise that people only act out according to their beliefs. It is better to enable others to correct their beliefs than to condemn their souls. Condemning a soul for his or her false beliefs is not beneficial to your own well-being.

Oh beloved, if everyone walked in the truth of their being, there would be no wrongdoing.

It is only from ignorance and fear that people act wrongly.

It is better to lead others into the light than to push them further into the darkness.

It is senseless to judge another if you are imprisoned by false thinking.

In judging another, you are only judging yourself because you and they are one.

You are no better than they. Instead of being quick to condemn another, look first to your own faults. You are responsible for your own actions and inactions, your own intentions. You need not judge a person's soul, but do not be indifferent to harmful actions. When you recognise a harmful behaviour, offer guidance from love rather than condemnation out of fear.

Hypocrites

For every person in your life, give thanks. Everybody has equal rights; everybody has a right to be here, for you are all of me and loved by me equally. Those who are doing wrong cannot see in their darkness; bring the light.

Be the light.

Be aware of my presence in everybody, even those you judge as undesirable. I *am* in them as love.

It is only your judgment that is undesirable.

Do not point your finger at another without first considering your own heart. Hypocrites are those who judge from a place of darkness. They have no clarity because they cannot see clearly without the light. All who are aware of their true nature and live in their truth see from my perspective. Hypocrites are still in the darkness.

You Are Not A Judge Of Souls

You are a divine soul; you are not a judge. Accept all others, because they are divine souls equally.

With acceptance of others comes a freeing in your spirit. Now as you encounter others, you have no need to judge, and thus by accepting them, you are kind to your own being. Judging brings a tension into your body, because the divinity within you, knowing you are all one, cringes, accepting judgment upon itself. This is felt as muscle tension and results in energy blockages within your being. Often the very thing you would condemn in another is found in some form in yourself. Look, then, within yourself, and become aware of your own behaviour and thoughts that are based in darkness. Bring them to the light, and free yourself from them. As you set yourself free from the darkness, you find that you become at ease with yourself, and the need to judge others dissipates into acceptance. Those still struggling in the darkness need light before they can see.

By judging, you deny yourself the gift of seeing yourself in others. The truth of your being resonates more than words.

When you notice others acting from their fear and darkness, use discernment. Perhaps you can help them. In this way, you are caring. Discernment from love without condemnation opens the heart for healing.

Thou shalt not judge any soul. Behaviour may be judged from love.

My Judgment

I *am* truth. I cannot judge what is not real. All that is real is perfect, needing no judgment. I do not judge. Atonement means at-one-ment. By knowing your true nature, you are reconciled to me in your belief structure. We are one, and our oneness is all. At-one-ment is your acceptance of the truth of our union.

I do not ask for payment for sin that is not real. Anything that is used as a means to deny our oneness, your true nature, is a falsity. Sin, therefore, is a falsity. In this way, you can determine the truth.

Many who are not conscious of their truth behave from their false beliefs. They are stuck only as long as they stay in the darkness. Since you are not body but spirit, you may use several bodies to achieve your goal of knowing yourself. You are your own judge and your self-judgments affect each of your lifetimes. Your acceptance of truth liberates you from your own judgments, enabling you to see them as part of the dream from which you have now woken.

Compassion Despite The Illusion

Your true nature is caring and compassionate.

Treat others as you would like to be treated in any situation. Be more aware and compassionate.

Give from your love; give not from fear.

Learn to see others through the eyes of your heart and soul rather than through the eyes of ego.

Beyond the external presentation of people is their soul, their truth, and their true nature. Communicate with their true nature.

Those living within their own darkness may project from fear. Reacting to their fear gives it validity, encasing them deeper in their illusion. The illusionary gap between darkness and truth widens as their fear is condoned.

Stay true to yourself. Know that others may yet be struggling in the darkness, and do not react to their illusion.

Do not react to their illusion because if you do, you are denying their truth. Look beyond the shadow. Responding to their truth, their true nature, gives it identity and validity. They recognise a part of themselves they had forgotten, and then they begin to remember. Many then begin to seek within themselves for alternative ways of being. By exploring their true nature and finding their authentic power, their fears cease to exist.

Be True To Soul

Stay true to your soul, to your own truth, showing others another way to find satisfaction and peace. Careers, possessions, money, and hobbies fall short in delivering the peace that only knowing your soul can bring.

Do not be like those who spend their whole lives moving houses, changing jobs, accumulating wealth and assets, and even raising children so they can feel satisfied with their life. All these things only give temporal satisfaction; the hunger within still remains.

Substances such as drugs and alcohol do little to fill the void. There are sometimes those who use the guise of anger to cover the void or those who become possessive of another being in an attempt to fill their own emptiness.

Real satisfaction is the satisfaction from communing with your own soul.

When you are complete in who you are, you need nothing or no one because you have everything within yourself.

At Home Within Your Being

Your home is within you. Wherever you go and whatever you are doing, you are at home within your being. You are at home within your being as you are attuned to your soul and to me. Your soul not only lives within you, but you are also encased within your soul. Coming home to your spiritual truths results in an epiphany of who you really are. Knowing the peace of soul means that you no longer need to seek for satisfaction externally, for you are completely satisfied within at all times. No longer striving to fulfil ego's needs, you are free to follow where your soul leads you. Not only are you free from striving for satisfaction, but you are also free from the condemnation of others and yourself. No longer are you affected by the criticism of others, and no longer do you feel the need to judge yourself. This freedom brings you a tremendous sense of well-being because you are reassured beyond any doubt that all is well.

All is well. Soul is in control of your life, and soul knows all and guides you in your best interest.

In this way you are led to higher ground, a higher vibration, a higher vantage point, and your higher self.

CHAPTER 5

The Realisation Of Spirit

Senses Of Spirit

As your consciousness expands, your vibration increases to a point where you sense beyond what you can physically perceive. The senses of your spiritual body are profoundly different from those of your physical body. Being of spirit, they do not need an organ to receive information. By identifying yourself with your true nature, that of spirit, you open yourself to the attributes of spirit. One of these is in the sensory dimension.

My breath is your being. I breathed you into being.

My Breath Is The Energy Of All

Each of you are energy, and within your being are energy portals enabling access to my energy of all. Increasing your vibration allows a better flow of energy from me to you and vice versa.

Your mere awareness of this increases it yet more. It is likened to removing a boulder from a stream. Awareness and appreciation help the flow of energy.

My energy flows in and through your being, carrying with it my perceptions based on truth.

You are a receptacle for knowledge beyond any knowledge perceived by your five senses.

You are a receptacle of my truths.

Sometimes you may hear without the use of your ears. Sometimes you may see without the use of your eyes. You may smell or taste without a physical source. You may know beyond all you have learnt. Learn to trust these spiritual insights, for they have been perceived in truth. You may receive knowledge regarding another person. Sometimes it is helpful if this knowledge is passed on to this person. Other times you may filter the insight and on the rare occasion withhold the knowledge completely.

At all times use discernment and be guided by your soul.

Attachment To Form

Know that you cannot carry the form you now take into eternity.

Your body is a unit made up of cells that accommodate your life force. Your life force is in constant motion, flowing throughout each cell of your body. Your life force is your spirit. All the cells of your body are interrelated, and the presence of your spirit is felt in each cell. The actual form in which you have manifested is limited in that it in itself has no mind.

You have a mind. Your mind is either succumbed to ego or aligned with spirit.

The body is directed by the mind of ego or by the mind of spirit. The mind of ego is a selfish mind, fearing its own demise. It does not feel responsible for the body out of love but out of fear. Your body is influenced by your thoughts, but I say to you that you are not *your* thoughts.

You are a spirit being, and when you claim your truth, you claim your oneness with me. As one, you live in me, and you are *my* thoughts. I express my being in your truth.

Your body is impermanent, but you, dear one, are eternal.

Be more concerned for your soul, which is eternal, than your perishable body.

Release yourself from the belief that you are your body. Release yourself from attachment to form. Release yourself from attachment to the roles you are playing.

Allow yourself to be one with me.

You Are Divine Energy

Feel yourself as my energy.

Know yourself as my energy.

As divine energy, you are without limits and freely walk this earth in the truth of your being.

Life on earth is not perfect and your bodies are not perfect, but all that is eternal is perfect. In that way, your true nature is perfection.

Bliss

Look within and know your true self, your soul; know me.

By choosing to follow soul, you lose naught but gain all.

Walking the divine path for your life offers you liberation from any snare that would bind you in false hopes.

After knowing such internal bliss, turning back to your old, limited nature is an undesirable option. Nothing the world can offer you can compare with what spirit can give you. The darkness of an unfulfilled, illusionary life cannot compare with the light of a bliss-filled life of truth.

Knowing who you are in truth, your true nature gives you an indication of what life is like for you when you leave your earthbound body. The feeling you have of completeness and bliss is magnified so many times more, and it cannot be described in any word it cannot be captured in any language. Your body is a limitation in that you take it with you, you feed it, you clothe it, and you are aware of it. Being one in spirit, you are aware of an ecstasy of being beyond anything that it could be compared to.

Do not fear the death of your body because it is only a vessel to bring you through life. Know that when you leave your body, you are back where you belong. It is very familiar to you. You are my sons and daughters. It is truth, I bring to you. It is love in which you are wrapped. It is grace in which you exist.

I love you. My love is all around you and within you.

Fear Is Not Real

Feel the love within your own soul; feel my love. The love you can perceive in your earthly form is miniscule compared to what you have awareness of in spirit form. Be afraid no more, for in my truth there is only love.

I *am* love. You also are love, but you do not realise the meaning of this. In love there is can be no fear. Therefore, in your truth, which is love, there can be no fear. Therefore, in you there can be no fear.

Fear is then not real when you are real.

When you take your true nature, you are real, and being real is not fear. Be bold, then, in your truth of soul. In your being within me, be bold, for you have nothing real to fear because fear is not real. Your true existence cannot be threatened because it is eternal. The light of your soul will never go out. In me you live, breathe, and have your being. In me you dwell, regardless of whether you are aware of this or not.

Holy Power

I say that if you know me then you know yourself as a part of me, claim your power, and do not underestimate the power within you. It is divine, it is love and it is yours. You have within you the power to heal and the power to perform miracles including manifestations, the power within you is almighty power. My power is within you. My strength is within you

Some may find their way to this power without acknowledging its source. They use the power to manifest without first knowing their souls. If only they would acknowledge their souls, it would be better for them. The use of your power without spirit makes the ego swell, increasing the illusion of separateness.

Knowing your soul does not take power from you; it adds to your power.

CHAPTER 6
The Discovery Of Self

Gaining All

Acknowledging that you are a part of me and that I reside in you is not a sign of weakness. On the contrary, it is a sign of wisdom. It is not that on finding me within, you surrender to me; on finding me within, you recognise your true nature, that you *are* one with me. You need only surrender your ego to your soul, and in doing that, you gain all.

My love for you is eternal. You dwell in my love eternally.

What Is Time in Eternity?

Time does not exist in eternity; it only exists in your perception of your physical reality. If your earth disappeared, the space that it was in has no time. Likewise, eternity existing in infinity has no time.

Time exists only in the matrix of your illusion.

You cannot imagine timelessness because, having free will, you chose to live your human existence within the limits of time. You could have just as easily chosen to live within your human existence as infinite beings. It is for this reason that time exists for you.

Knowing your own greatness, you chose an experience that needed confines as you chose not to experience your humanness forever.

You believe that time exists purely on your experience of change. You notice that everything is in a constant state of change. Change is motion. Observing time requires some factor of motion. Without motion of any sort, you are unaware of time passing. This motion may be in terms of day and night hours, growth in living things, your digestive system working, or a clock, but without motion, you cannot have time. This is because you can only observe time as it passes. If it did not move, it would be timeless.

I *am* timeless, my love is timeless, and your true being is timeless. Eternity is timeless. Eternity is beyond the illusion of time.

Illusion

Your bodies are a limitation; they are an illusion

Time is a limitation; it is an illusion

Separation from the reality of oneness is a limitation; it is an illusion.

Set yourself free by choosing to wake up. Wake up—no illusion, no limitations.

Bonded In Spirit

There are no strangers. Each person is your brother or sister in grace. You are connected to all by a spiritual bond that is far greater than any physical bond you may have, even within your own family.

The bonds you have with your family are genetic, but in spirit, the bonds between souls are much greater because you are all one.

No soul is loved more than another, because it would not be possible to love one part more than another. In me you are all complete, all loved, and all one. Know yourself, know me, and in doing so, you know all persons. Reach out and refuse no one, for you are all parts of the one. Do not withhold help of any sort to anyone in need. See everyone as your equal.

I Am In All

Beloved, my spirit resides in every being. Therefore, as you do unto others, you do to me. Because of this, even interrupting a person is felt as denying the worth of that person.

Even if you are not interested in what the person is saying, be interested in the person.

Value others, listen to them, and consider them. Be compassionate to all others. Do not judge them by the role they are playing. Know that in spirit you are one.

I *am* in your darkness, and I *am* in your light. There is nowhere that I *am* not. I *am* in *all*.

The Soul Is Innocent

So many look for me in their minds and in the wisdom of others, but I say use your minds and the wisdom of others, but only *you* can know your soul. Only by knowing your trueness can you forsake this illusion and come home. Look inside, and think of yourself as a little child. Remember that in your soul you are innocent, beyond judgment, and beyond guilt. You are taking in the world around you like a big sponge, absorbing information. Remember the way you viewed life. You thought you could do anything or be anyone. Your soul was pure and untarnished. Being soul, you identified with all life, recognising yourself in it. You saw yourself as a part of all, and being that part, you allowed yourself to be influenced, adopting the biases of your parents and others who were significant adults in your life. In so doing, you accepted those feelings of guilt, learnt to judge, and became less aware of your god nature. Is it any wonder so many of you have a battle with worthiness?

Remember your soul, remember yourself.

As a little child, you remembered, and so you felt secure, you trusted, and you loved unconditionally. As a child, you didn't realise that you had a choice—a choice to remain intimate with your spirit truths or to identify with feelings and beliefs that were not true. As a baby, you were influenced by the adults in your life who in turn were influenced by theirs. You chose the path of separateness and fear rather than of soul and love, and in so doing, you removed the memory of your true being from yourself. The memory may have gone, but the proof of your origin is coded within your DNA. It is also encoded in the DNA of everything else that lives in your planet of illusion.

The Object of the Game of Life Is to Find Yourself

When the allowed time is up in your experiment, events will orchestrate themselves to such a degree in your world that all will know the truth. This will be two-fold. The evidence will establish the proof that as above, so below. This evidence will be clear and beyond refutation. It will establish that my consciousness is in all, and it will link my energy to the truths in your DNA.

The two simultaneously become known, meaning that mankind will reveal the nature of the above at the same time as revealing the secret held in your DNA.

This also means that your experiment to live in harmony with nature, acknowledging the source of all for your existence and co-relationships with others, failed within the guidelines of the experiment. Citing such evidence may be compared to cheating by looking up the answers in the back of a book. The only reason one would possibly cheat is if all other means for reaching the answer appeared unobtainable. The fact that you use science to prove the truth of *all* is irrelevant. All that matters is that you find your way home.

Faith leads you to the answer unscientifically within your very soul. It is so obvious that many are blind to it.

All that matters is that you accept the truth into your being. Know the truth about yourself, and as you do, you know the truth of *all*.

CHAPTER 7

The Symbolism Of Christ

Jesus-Sacrifice For Sin

Jesus came to help set the record straight; you interpreted him wrong based on the opinions of others. He came because you denied your true nature and believed yourselves to be unworthy of me. This denial of yourself meant you then saw yourself as separate from me. Since you could not be separate from me as I am in you, you had to find some reason for this manmade separation. That reason, you agreed, was to be called sin. In actual fact, sin does not exist because you are all me and I am without flaw.

Sin is a creation of your mind. It stems from the illusion of separateness.

Jesus came to free you from sin and separateness. He played along with your illusion in the hope that by destroying him, you would free yourself from this deception. However in destroying him, many of you alienated yourselves even further by identifying with the crucifixion rather than the symbolism, which is all that it was.

Separated By Sin

Jesus was the symbol of sin. His death meant that sin no longer existed.

Behold my innocent lamb that took away the sin of the world. Your perceived sins were laid on Jesus. You no longer have that as a reason for your state of supposed separateness. You can now acknowledge that without sin there was no separateness, but you took the stance that you helped crucify Christ by being sinners and so separated yourselves even further by embedding yourselves within this belief. You saw the crucifixion as symbolic of forgiveness rather than symbolic of sin. You identified yourselves as sinners who can only reconnect with me through forgiveness. In that way, you keep yourselves separate, and you keep me outside of yourselves.

How I long for you to see the truth that I am a part of you, not apart from you.

No Sin—No Separation

When Jesus said, "Repent, the kingdom of heaven is at hand," you took it to mean, "Be sorry and ask forgiveness because my kingdom is coming to reign on earth." That was two thousand years ago. That's a long time for those who are waiting.

Jesus did not get it wrong; you interpreted it wrong. When Jesus said repent, it meant "have a change of mind." When he said the kingdom of heaven was near, he meant that he was soon to be crucified. Therefore, the perceived sins that kept you separate from me would be gone. He was telling you to change your mind because there would soon be no separation. The kingdom of heaven was within you all the time, very close at hand. Jesus was symbolically the bridge between deception and truth. The only way he could lead you to cross the water of deception, was by being part of your world, part of your illusion. He was in the world but not of the world. By becoming the symbol of sin, he led you across the bridge to truth.

Read the holy books again from the perspective that you are part of me and that the only separation that ever existed between us was the illusion you held in your mind.

Think about Krishna, Buddha, Jesus, Allah, and all other gods.

It is by opening your minds and your hearts that you understand that religions are founded on what is believed to be true for those gods. My truth is beyond belief, it is a knowing. Religions are man's attempt at defining god in a way they can relate to. Know that the truth sets you free from the need to define, for all is as it is. The true knowledge of your being knows no boundaries of definition.

Sacrifice

To those who prostrate themselves in adoration of me, I say rise up. Do you not know I dwell within you? It is not the sacrifice of your body offered on the altar of your prayers that I want. I want to commune with you. I want you to honour our relationship.

I *am* in you, and you are in me. We are intimate, although you know it not.

Understand yourself. In that way you understand the source you are a part of. Recognise yourself, your true nature, for it is only by this that you will come to truly commune with me.

Your true nature is *my* nature. You are light, you are love, and you are one with all. You are both in me and in yourself. You are above and below, as am I.

Commune with me, and work to help others recognise their truth. In that way, you use your body for your own service because we are one.

Rise up. Do not offer your life as a sacrifice to me by your prayers. Your life is better used to service mankind for the good of all.

Rise up, open yourself to your soul, and commune with me. I *am* with you always. When you are sleeping and when you are awake, I *am* there. I cannot leave a part of myself. You are that part.

Go forth; go forth into the world with your light.

Commune with me within the sanctuary of your soul.

Games

There have been many games played on your earth. Each has had its own set of rules; the object of each game was always the same: to find yourself. Do not become so obsessed with the rules of the game, believing that conforming to rules is your way to salvation. This is mere stupidity.

It is better to release yourself from the rules that bind you and find your true nature than to bind yourself in the rules and deny your true nature.

When you come back to yourself, you need no rules because you *are* love.

Seek to know who you really are.

Choose to move from the rule of ego to the realm of soul.

Those who refuse to claim their truth play the game of life according to the rules over and over again. There are always clues in each game that point you within, but many disregard the clues or deny the importance of them. Do you become love and light by knowing the rules? If you must stick to the rules, the true message is encoded within them. Look for the clues. Look within. Your soul is eternally present and contains your truth. Find it, know yourself, and know me.

You are omniscient; your body is not. You are eternal; your body is just your shell. When you leave it, it decays because its purpose is over. You all ultimately share the same destiny: oneness in glory.

Symbolism

When Jesus hung on the cross and said, "Father forgive them for they know not what they do," he was implying that you still believed in sin and separateness regardless of his teachings. He was not implying that you were sinners for crucifying him. Much of his teaching that was an example of how living within spirit could and should have been for you was brushed off as symbolic, and the symbolism of the crucifixion was taken as literal.

In this way, the life of Jesus and the Bible have been used by those in false power to perpetrate the myth.

The Base Of Power—Truth Or Lies

There are those of you who have become obsessed with self-power, which is fine if it is based in truth, but when it is based in the deception and lies that your illusion has created, it is misleading and dangerous to others of you who want to find your inner truth and your way home.

The healings and miracles Jesus performed were living examples of how life in the spirit should be. They were not to prove that he was the son of God. Jesus was a son of mine, as you are sons and daughters. He came to earth in the same fleshy body, and he had the same soul as you. The difference was that he retained his awareness of who he was. He held his awareness of who he was regardless of the influences of others around him. He called you his brothers and sisters, he taught you righteous living, and he taught you how to use the power within you. He taught you how to pray.

The Lord's Prayer is communion between us *acknowledgment* of our relationship (me in you and you in me; together one).

The Lord's Prayer

"Our Father"—Jesus was saying he was the same as you. He had the same relationship with me that you have. I *am* your father.

"Who art in heaven"—heaven is infinite. It includes your hearts.

"Hallowed be thy name"—when you listen within, you hear the still, small voice of truth. I am truth. It is hallowed, and it does not proclaim its powers by shouting.

"Thy kingdom come thy will be done on earth as it is in heaven"—realise that when you know our true selves, you will do my will, the divine will, because that is who you truly are, and you will see the kingdom within yourself and earth as part of heaven.

"Give us this day our daily bread"—live in the present. That doesn't suggest that I feed you for the future. At each moment, your needs are taken care of as you trust in your true self.

"Forgive us our trespasses as we forgive them that trespass against us"—There is no sin, only the false belief that you are all separate. The need for forgiveness disappears as light entering the darkness vanishes. False beliefs turn into nothingness. It is only then from the perspective of truth that you can acknowledge your old nature as part of the illusion.

"Lead us not unto temptation"—it has never been spirit that tempts you. Only in illusion does ego keep you further from the truth. Sometimes your soul allows you to get yourselves into situations, knowing that there are lessons to be learnt.

"Deliver us from evil"—the only evil is fear, which comes from ignorance of who you are. You deliver yourself from this as you set yourself free from false beliefs.

"For thine is the kingdom, the power and the glory forever and ever, amen"—Thine! You are a part of me, and therefore, all this is yours. Amen! This prayer that is known as the Lord's Prayer is a declaration of your union with me. This is a verbal acknowledgment of your own power.

Know yourself; to your own self be true.

Jesus Christ came to save your souls, to set you free from the law by offering you his spirituality. Many, frightened that liberation would cause anarchy, contained the Christ within the law, calling it religion.

But I say unto you: spirituality is freedom from the delusion of religion. You either follow your spirit or follow man.

CHAPTER 8

The Power Of Thought

False Identity

My love, have you ever felt like a failure? Have you ever felt like you were not good enough? Every negative identity that you ever owned was not you.

You were never a failure. You were always good enough.

These negative impressions you gave yourself were just that—an impression. These impressions were perceived from ego's falseness. In reality, they never existed. It was only your belief in them that gave them any power. You believed the lies that ego told you, but I am truth. The truth will set you free from false identities. These false identities have been like a dirty garment that you have worn because you didn't realise you could change your clothes.

Take off that dirty garment, and put on the robe of truth.

You focus on the fears, which obscure your true self, but realising that these fears only exist in your mind and they are false, you are able to see through them because they no longer contain any substance. You are able to recognise your own truth.

You are worthy, you are important, and your life makes a difference to the world. Watch your life unfold as you live your purpose.

As you step into the light, the darkness recedes from your mind, and the dream vanishes—only a distant memory.

Coincidence

Many of you now are becoming reconciled with spirit; you are noticing synchronicities in your life appearing frequently, like signs appearing before you even need them. These synchronicities are partly of your own doing. They are manifested vibrationally as your spirit comes into alignment. The more synchronicities in your life, the more you become aware of the web of illusion in which you exist. You are becoming in sync with me. Coincidences in your life are a way of making you pay attention. The next time you find a coincidence in your life, know that there is something about that situation that has triggered a response. It is up to you to interpret the incident correctly. As your ways are attuned to my ways, the incidents of coincidence may increase; take heed.

Sometimes even your desires can bring elements synchronistically together. Do you recall an incident when you were thinking about someone and then all of a sudden you met him or her? Such is the power of your thought. Coincidences happen like this all the time, pointing you to your own power. But time and time again you take no notice. You brush these off as some force beyond your control, negating your own power.

Be aware; learn that the power resides within you to draw things together.

When you resist the acknowledgment your own power, you deny yourself the satisfaction of transforming your life through directed thought.

Intent is a key factor in coincidence; it is the intent in focused thought that initiates the flow of synchronicity in your life. It is when you make the connection between yourself and these seemingly coincidental events that you recognise the synergy of manifestation.

Faith Triggers The Energy Of What Is To Come

Often there are several steps before the final outcome is achieved. You are often only aware of the first and last stage of the synchronistic process. You are aware that you had an initial thought, and you are aware of the thing you thought about somehow appearing in your life. You do not have to be aware of the process involved to make that happen. But there was a process, finely tuned to deliver the optimum outcome at the perfect time.

Once you are aware that when you release your intentions, they are then taken up by my energy and given back to you in the appropriate form, you will let your intentions go free instead of worrying about them.

As long as you hold an intention and as long as you worry over something, I cannot help you. Have faith, let it go, and be awake to the result.

Faith triggers the energy of what is to come.

Of course it helps if you have clarity in your intention because being vague instigates only scattered energy. Scattered energy is weak compared to a strong jet of energy focused in its direction. If you really want a result, release a strong, focused thought into my space, and let me deal with it. Listen to your soul, follow its guidance, and all will be revealed. Be in tune with the rhythm of life's song, and be conscious of every moment. Go with the flow of life, and get in "sync" with me. When you do, the timing of the whole universe matches yours. As above, so below.

I *am* the space wherein all is created. I *am* all space. I *am* the eternal presence. There is nowhere that I am not. There is nothing that I cannot do. With me all things are possible. I am within you, and you reside in me.

Your Soul Exists In Other Dimensions

There are different realms existing within your reality, and this is due to different vibrations. The reality you are in now is the dream you have chosen to be in. There are other segments of your soul within other dreams. Just as I exist in spirit everywhere, you also have fragmented your soul to experience different dreams. You are unaware of your hologram, but on waking from your dream, you are once more united.

You are a soul, a pure essence of me. Your soul is your very being. In me you live, breathe, and have your being. In you I live, breathe, and have my being. In you I *am*. In me, you are beyond self.

Take down the barriers. Let your soul go free, knowing it is safe within me.

Waking up awakes your consciousness. Be conscious in all your actions and inactions. Inactions are thoughts. Be conscious in your thoughts.

Thoughts

Thoughts are energy, and so they can be transformed from one form of energy to another.

Thought channels small elemental particles that are resonating at high frequency. They have the ability to alter their frequency and become the manifestation of their imagined vision.

Energy cannot be created or destroyed. It can be turned from one form to another, however. Everything is energy, and everything is infinite, so energy comes from an infinite source. When you imagine, you draw on the infinite energy to create a picture in your mind using thought energy. You then release this picture, which is then vibrating in the ether. Having faith, believe that you have already received it, and it will come to you. Under the law of attraction, like attracts like, so an image vibrating within the ether attracts its likeness. Thereby it attracts its manifestation. The more feeling energy attached to the image, the greater its power of attraction.

In other words, act according to your faith, believing that you have already received. This law of attraction can be used negatively, which so many of you do because you are not aware of the power of your own thought. How often do you view yourselves negatively? I know you often think, *I'm too fat, too short, and too ugly. I haven't got enough money or friends,* or any number of negative thoughts. These negative thoughts quickly become images in your mind and immediately begin their manifestation process. In that way, you can create your own reality.

Being Conscious

You are of my creative soul. You are creators in your own right, but conscious creation for good is what you need to be focusing your thoughts on. Those of you who are awake can use your thought energy for the good of the planet. Imagine everyone living in harmony with each other and nature. Imagine an awareness of others rising to recognise their truth, knowing they are one with me.

Be conscious of your actions, even your eating. If you are consciously aware of all that you eat, you will maintain a healthy body because you will only eat what your body requires. Be conscious of your dealings with others, remembering your thoughts can be just as powerful as your actions. Your thoughts form your identity. It is correct that what you think determines who you have come to be. Many of you have been slaves to your thoughts, believing in things that were told to you as children. For example, you may have been told or had reason to think many years ago that you were no good, you were overweight, you lacked confidence, or you were scared of the dark and you have held onto these beliefs. You held onto these beliefs and created an identity for yourself around them.

Know that these beliefs are only there because you didn't realise that you had a choice; that you could accept them or refuse them.

Imagination Creates Circumstances

You came to this earth as an innocent soul. Your conscious mind was a blank canvas, and within you lay the ability to make yourself into any type of person you imagined you could be. The key word is imagine, because from that imagination of yours comes belief. Even if you were in an environment that was 99 percent positive, many of you would dwell on that 1 percent that was negative; a not-so-flattering remark or something similar became the focus of your thoughts. The good news is that you can still use your creative powers to change your thoughts, which in time change your identity. From now on, choose only positive thoughts. Imagine yourself in the way you wish to be, and behave the way you would if you were the image in your mind. Before long, the positive image in your mind becomes your new reality. You create the circumstances of your life.

Ruling Your Mind

You are one with me, yet you are unique. Each one of you is special and loved beyond measure. Oh if only you would stop hurting yourselves by your negative thinking and be the person within your power to be. From now on, choose to rule your mind rather than letting your mind rule you. If you have made a choice to follow the path of your soul, your soul will help you to do this effectively. It is that simple. In fact, everything is simple.

Ruling your mind is just a matter of making a decision, that decision being to take charge. This is extremely powerful and will again lead you to another choice to use your mind wisely for good or to use it unwisely for the detriment of this world. Know that whatever you think about another, you are really thinking about yourself because we are all one. Judge not, because when you judge others, you are judging yourself. Love others as you love yourself means that you cannot love anyone else until you truly learn to love yourself, for in fact you are one.

CHAPTER 9

The Connection To Soul

Love Yourself

Recognise The Voice Of Soul

Waking Up

Being In Touch

False Teachers

Materialism Does Not Satisfy The Soul

Love Yourself

Loving yourself is not to be seen as vanity but as a prerequisite to love in total. Begin to love yourself. See yourself through the eyes of your soul. Know me in you, feel my love for you, and refresh your love for yourself. It is there, buried under all your negativity. You will find it by making the choice to. When you look at others, even strangers, you will begin to witness a wave of compassion for them, as truly loving yourself is the catalyst for this. This feeling of compassion that you feel for others in turn starts a reaction within them as they, feeling that love, begin to love themselves, and so the cycle increases. Sometimes loving yourself comes before knowing me, but as you love yourself, you begin to know yourself, and in doing so, you find me within you. Other times the awakening to this dream is needed before you acknowledge who you truly are, and then loving yourself comes with understanding that knowledge.

Honour your life, honour the life of all things living, and honour the energy of all nonlife.

Recognise The Voice Of Your Soul

Within your heart abides your soul. Its murmurings are often hushed by the other, louder voices of your being. These voices are in your head. Still your mind until you are free of thought and just be. Be mindful of your inner being, and listen to your soul. If you listen to the voice of your heart, you will recognise it as the voice of love, truth, and divine knowledge. Your ego would have you listen to the voices in your head that try to outdo each other for your attention. My voice, your soul voice, is found within your heart. It is so easy to hear if you would only just listen.

Take time to be quiet, and take time for inner reflection.

The voices in your head are convincing. They come as a wolf in sheep's clothing. They are of ego and are a deceiving part of your plan of forgetfulness. Listen to them if you choose to carry on with your game of separateness. There has been much interest in the law of attraction and the law of manifestation, but if these do not point to your soul through grace, they are not of me.

Waking Up

Your authentic power is found in your soul, not in your mind. Unless you are soul conscious, your miracles of healing and manifestation are the ego playing at being the angel of light, keeping you in the illusion of separateness awhile longer.

Know the God in yourselves, take down your invisible walls, and let the light shine forth from within your soul to others caught still in the web they have woven. When the light of truth hits their web, it disappears as darkness does when light hits it.

When you recognise the voice of your soul, you sense the liberation at hand and are often overwhelmed by the beauty you find within. It is a relief to wake from your dream. It is a relief to find your life suddenly makes sense. You realise you were safe all along. I long for you to wake from this dream. I long for you to put an end to your self-inflicted suffering. It is then our holy communion begins.

Grace is light that draws you near to me and further from illusion; truth is the perfume of soul that entices you in your search for what was once obvious but now lies hidden in ego's game.

Being In Touch

You have the choice to continue in this game of struggle you call life or to awaken to your spirit within. A dream does not compare with the reality of soul—your soul, my soul, the oneness of our being, eternally beautiful. Sometimes when you sit in my presence, you wish you could experience those feelings longer, and you would if something from your illusionary world did not drag you back into your game. Becoming your authentic self, seeing yourself in me and vice versa brings with it the awareness of what is divine truth—that peace that surpasses anything your illusionary world could offer. You inherently know this feeling. It is in you. It is being in touch with your soul, and nothing in your dream compares, so you know there is more to life than this dream, and so you seek.

You seek until you find within your soul your true nature. For many of you, this lifetime is the one in which you have predetermined to finish your game, but for many that game has become so real that they doubt their actual origin. So your soul, keeping its part of the contract, allows things to happen that bring you often to a crisis point, forcing you to evaluate your life and suggesting a change in direction. Still, some do not heed the prompting of soul. For some the nudges soul gives increase to a point where you have to notice. Others leave this life without an awareness of their true being, to be born yet again into this wheel that turns, offering falseness and suffering until they choose to get real and be one with me again.

False Teachers

There are many offering to help you find your way. Be careful who you choose to follow because many of these helpers are just pawns to sustain the game you created. There are many offering wisdom, but if their wisdom does not vibrate within you as truth, touch it not. There are many who profess that there is only one way to truth, that only by believing in certain prophets or performing certain rituals can you know me.

There is only one way to know me, and that is to know yourself as I am in you. It is a waking a realisation of who you are, but there are many ways to come to this waking point, be it through teachers, books, rituals, meditations, or nature. All are instrumental in pointing you back to your true nature. It is knowing the truth that sets you free and that lets you see the illusion. Once you see through the great illusion, your only desire is that others would find their way also. That being so, you become as beacons, and through your witness, others may choose to follow.

Materialism Does Not Satisfy The Soul

Even though some are faced with the truth, they will choose still to deny it, doubting the unseen and preferring the tangible, materialistic objects within which they have placed their trust. These materialistic objects may be satisfying for the ego but not for the soul. Many trust these false objects to give them satisfaction, peace, and worth, and in them they place their salvation. They do not know that these things will pass away like chaff blown by the wind.

In this way, the true nature of all things is nothing. All that you consider your possessions, do not exist in reality.

The security of an empire built from ego cannot compare with the peace gained from the security of trusting your soul. Things and possessions know not how to give real satisfaction and real peace, nor can they match a person's worth. There is always a void that cannot be denied and can only by filled by your acknowledgment of my spirit within yourself.

CHAPTER 10

The End Of The Dream

Realisation At Time Of Death

Always Safe

A Waking Dream

Acceleration Of Vibration

Nothing Is Constant Except My Love

Perceiving Beyond Form

Realisation At Time Of Death

Sometimes you may bear witness to one who is successful in the eyes of your illusionary world who, upon being faced with death, realises that all his worldly possessions account for nothing. All he wants is the inner peace that evaded him while he put his faith outside of his soul. Even in his dying, he can choose to see through the illusion. Some do. Others don't and try to cling to life and their things as their spirits leave their bodies. It is these who come back and back to suffer time and time again because of their pride, their greed, or their low self-worth (believing themselves to be sinners), denying their souls the riches of the eternal kingdom. It is these ones for whom there is much rejoicing when they do come into their truth. These are the lost sheep; I am the keeper of souls.

It is not wise to devote your life to things of no substance. Why grasp for what is not permanent and deny what is? Recognise the impermanent illusions in your life. Upon that recognition, the illusion shatters. When you recognise the nature of your soul, the truth is revealed.

Always Safe

Know that your souls are always kept safe, even when you choose to live in denial of me. They cannot be anything but safe, for everything is in me. You are forever in my bosom. It is just that many of you still sleep. In your sleep, you dream that you are separate from me and also from every other living thing. When you wake, you will see how foolish your dream was. You are in me. You are in everything because you are a part of me and I am omnipresent, as are you. The very essence of me that is within your soul is in the soul of every other. In that way, you also are in them. We are one. The oneness that you talk of becoming you are already. We are forever one. Only the fact that you are unaware that you are sleeping causes you to imagine that you are not yet a part of that oneness, that union with me. And so it is that there are those who are now waking to bring the awareness into the minds of those who still sleep.

A Waking Dream

As you walk within the light of your awareness, you no longer see darkness because you are no longer asleep, but many will still see the dream, although recognising it to be just that—a dream. You are aware that the life you live is a dream. You are participating in your own dream. It is a waking dream. You are aware that you are within the source of all and that others in your dream are still sleeping. Those who will be roused will wake to experience the light with you. Together you will see through the illusion.

Acceleration of Vibration

As more and more of you awake to your true natures, there will be acceleration in the rate of those who are waking up. This acceleration is caused by the increase in your vibration, which affects everything around you as you are connected to the all; you are one with the all. Just as the light from two little candles merge to make a light greater than the power of two separate candles, so too will your lights merge, and as they do, the light becomes so great that the darkness of unawareness that has held those sleeping, dissipates. Those of you who have woken are in the light or enlightened and will begin to see through the illusion. Matter may not appear to be solid, and you will experience instances where you can physically see objects of solid matter become objects of moving energy—vibrating molecules.

Nothing Is Constant Except My Love

Nothing is set solid. Observe life changing around you. Nothing is permanent. Everything is moving; everything changes. Only my love is constant. Relationships, people, the weather, and even landforms are all subject to change. Your values will change. No longer do you attribute worth to things that are perishable and illusions formed by dreaming. You value the truth in life. You have compassion for all life, knowing it is precious a part of yourself with its place in the scheme of things—a part of our grand design. You appreciate the life force within even the smallest insect. Every living thing is interrelated, but the form in which you see it with your physical eyes is as a mirage. This may be hard for you to understand, but do not be like those locked in close-minded dogma. Open your minds in your search for truth.

Many base their whole lives on a belief, and fearing the unmasking of that belief, they close their minds to all else.

Beloved, if your belief is unmasked as false, that does not mean your life will collapse. On the contrary, your life will expand in the fullness of truth. This is what is meant by being liberated. Closed minds equate to a life of limits. Truth releases you to a life exceeding all limits. It is only you who can choose the way in which you perceive as the basis for your life. I implore you look at your emotions, find your core beliefs, and match them to the truth of truths. If you are so sure your beliefs are based in truth, then what is to be feared in analysing them?

Know yourself; know me. I *am not* closed minded. I *am not* a God of limits. I *am* freedom, I *am* energy, I *am* truth, and I *am* love.

Perceiving Beyond Form

Every living thing is energy. As you recognise this, you cease to be attached to the form that you view. In that way, you identify with love for the energy, regardless of the appearance of form. Your perception of form arouses emotions in your being. Follow these emotions back to their origin. Look even behind the origin to find your core and reveal your inner truths. You can yield to emotion, or you can use it to explore your inner self. Emotions direct you to your core beliefs, and sometimes your beliefs are wrong. However, as you discover truths, your beliefs change. As you swap false beliefs for those grounded in truth, your emotions become more consistent.

It is the knowledge of the true nature of all that gives you emotional freedom because you are no longer attached to any form. All are equal; all are one. Oh beloved, these may seem like hard concepts to understand, but if you could only but accept them in faith, you would come into such an understanding of them that all would appear so simple.

The only form is what is perceived by your senses.

Your senses send messages to your brain, and you react to the information with your programmed emotion. Your senses are being replaced by spiritual perception as your frequencies increase; this is your natural next stage. By entering this stage, you perceive beyond form. There are some of you who are already beginning to glimpse the moving reality because things are now beginning to appear less solid. These are not times to be feared but to be anticipated for the harmony they bring.

CHAPTER 11

The Wisdom Of Nature

Connecting With Nature

You begin to feel your connection to the trees, grass, and flowers and realise that they came into being to support your dream existence and that often in that dream they were treated without regard, even though without them there would be no balance. Recognise the creation of nature, and know that all nature was formed for your benefit, even the weeds. Appreciate that all of nature contains within it a life-force—my spirit. You were formed by divine love, as was every aspect of nature. The same love that created them created you, and by creating, you became a part of me just as they are.

All of nature is included in this oneness. Nothing is separate. All are part of the whole. There will be those of you who, upon waking, find that your chosen professions are no longer compatible with your beliefs. You may recognise your affinity with other life to the extent that positions involving destruction or violation of animals or plants will seem abhorrent to you. This is a sign of your heart waking up, a sign of recognising the true spirit within nature. Animals and plants respond to you on the level of spirit. This is the true meaning of your dominance over them. As you respect them and communicate with them on the level of spirit, you will get the sense of them responding to you. Your spirit is linked intrinsically with theirs. Learn to ask them questions, and then within your heart feel their answer. This is how they communicate. This is natural communication the way it was meant to be.

All Nature Is Based In Me

Your consciousness with all of nature is based in me. In your dream state, so many of you chose to feel power rather than love, and this power was misused as you became deeper one with illusion. Many of the animals have become conditioned to disrespect, but they are not dreaming. For them the shift in you is enough to help release that conditioning. Their senses are more acute than yours, and they can sense love and respect before it is even spoken. Enjoy your friendship with nature, and be grateful for all she provides. Even as you take a life, be it an animal or a tree, if you need it for your physical survival, your gratefulness is what is felt. Your intent with right feeling, respect, love, and appreciation is so much different than no feeling, no respect, no love, and no appreciation for spirit.

Do not take a life of another creature or plant without thinking. Be conscious in all your actions regarding the welfare of others. If you can sidestep a mere earthworm on the footpath, it matters to that worm. See life from the perspective of other forms, and recognise their truth. They are true; nature in all her beauty is true. You know an ant acts like an ant. It is true to form. A tree is a tree, not capable of malice; sadness yes, malice no. A dog either likes you or it doesn't, and it tells you so. That is nature: harmony, balance, and being willing to bend to compromise the effect of humankind. Waking up the planet's balance is restored. Your true relationship with nature is symbiotic, a mutually beneficial agreement. It is the belief that each being is a separate entity that created the unbalance. Nature's beauty is for your appreciation. You care-take, and nature provides. There is enough sustenance in nature for the whole of mankind if managed correctly. There is no need for artificial food.

Nature's Wealth

Natural foods were made specifically for the needs of the human body. Do you not think that I would create your body and all the amazing systems within it without providing the resources to keep your body at its optimum performance capabilities?

You may be able to genetically clone some things in nature, but you will never genetically clone a soul.

Nature in her pure state is abundant. Every protein, mineral, and vitamin your body needs is found there. The trace elements your body needs are found in just the right proportions in a diet of balanced natural foods. Your bodies are capable of synthesizing substances so that they can attain the maximum benefit from them. Your bodies were created to run on pure, unadulterated foods, water, and oxygen. Natural resources are being abused. Their worth is not recognised. Instead you value processed, artificial foods. Is it any wonder you are having problems with your bodies?

Pollution

Water, air, and soil pollution not only affect humans but all life. If each of you cleaned up your own backyards, so to speak, and took some responsibility to help the neighbourhoods in which you live, the whole world would change. You care-take the earth by becoming more attentive to your surroundings, disposing of rubbish, protecting the flora and fauna, contributing to the well-being of others, and in general viewing mother earth as alive and respecting her. Literally speaking it is the earth that provides all that you need. All organic and inorganic elements originate from the earth. Your body takes its requirements from the food you eat. Be it animal or vegetable, the source of sustenance is the earth. The earth provides for my creation. I created her for that purpose. The ignorance of a few and the blasé attitude of many have caused the earth to be poisoned over much of her surface, including the waterways and air within her circumference. It is in your own best interest that you concern yourself with the wellness of the earth. In your own small way, be aware of all you put into the earth. If it seems to be toxic, use your resourceful mind and find some other means of disposing of it. The earth reciprocates the care you extend to her by providing for you.

Connecting To Earth

Connect with the earth. Many of you are starting to do this by imagining yourselves grounded to her (earthed). You may also be imagining roots growing downward through the earth, joining you to it. This is all part of your awareness as you begin to wake up to soul. When you consider the earth, you see perfection even in the weather patterns. She is a divine creation with all her systems—weather, tides, and so on—and all her formations—lakes, mountains, and oceans, to name a few. See her splendour, and know she is a gift to you. All earth's systems work compatibly, one with the other. Have you ever marvelled at the way people acquire fresh water from oceans of salty water? The sun causes water in the great oceans to evaporate; it is taken up as vapour and precipitated down to earth as fresh water in the form of rain. This rain is then processed to give you drinkable water. There are so many natural systems and processes, each one perfect. The earth moves in rhythm to the beat of the universe.

Your Body

Your bodies are temples of the living God. They house part of your soul, but you are not your body. You are without form; your bodies hold a portion of your divine nature.

You chose to come to earth in the constraint of form. You are then responsible for the care of your body. Give your body what it needs to function at its utmost efficiency. The body you are now in is the one you have chosen to be in for the lessons you have chosen to learn. Your body is your manifested form to get you through this lifetime. Your body needs proper nourishment from natural foods, and it needs fresh water, clean air, and exercise. If correct nourishment were given to your body it would be healthier—simple. So many of you abuse your bodies, you do not respect them. If you have any problems with your body, begin to love yourself.

Your earthly self includes your body, so love your body. Love your mind; think positively. Love your body; keep it healthy. Love your spirit; commune with your soul. Doing these three things will ensure that you have the best body for your life. Your mind, body, and soul are all part of this earthly adventure you have chosen. To love everything about yourself, learn to know yourself, for it is only then that you can love yourself completely. When you are able to love yourself in your entirety completely, your physical body responds to love, allowing grace to move. Grace then flows throughout your mind, your body, and your soul, beginning the process of transformation by increasing your vibration.

Vibration Affects Cells

The quickened vibration of your being can alter your body at a cellular level as your energy centres become activated and vibrate in unison with the joy of oneness. The changes in your body at cellular level move upward. Your organs, skeleton, and even external characteristics of your body are affected. Your earthbound body may weigh the same as before, but there is a feeling of lightness. This is due to the increased vibration as you identify more with your spiritual nature.

Healings, insights, miracles, and synchronicity come from a realm of higher vibration than your earth body. You move into this realm as you walk in the way of your soul.

If you walk in the way of your soul, you let grace flow in your life. Come walk with me, for I *am* the way of your soul.

Body Systems

Your body consists of many systems, all created to work in harmony to enable you to function better that any machine you could imagine. Have you ever wondered why even before you polluted the earth, your body had systems in place to filter toxins? Not only the hairs in your nose but also whole organs, such as the liver, are designed to reduce toxins entering your body systems. When your form was created, every last detail was put in place. You are perfect in your design. Although we are one, you are a complete individual. Honour yourself. Attune your mind to your body, and listen to your body. You are my beloved. As beautiful as the earth is, she was fashioned for you, and she will pass away, but your souls will not pass away, for they are one with me.

Want nothing, seek nothing, be complete in nothing, and be nothing.

I have no needs, for I am complete. As you become one with me, you too have no needs. You too are complete.

CHAPTER 12

The Delight In Being

Trust

Appreciate Each Day

Maintain A Disposition Of Gratitude

Grace

Look Within

Selfish Desires

The Ultimate Experience

Angels

Trust

My wisdom is beyond your comprehension. My wisdom created the systems through which you live—your body system, your earth system, the system of the universe—and yet you withhold your trust in me to guide your life, preferring to guide your life through the brain I formed.

Everything changes. To be attached to what changes is foolishness. Holding onto attachments is like grasping at reeds in a stream; let go. Go with the flow, dance with life, and move in me.

Trying to exert control over what is not yours to control is foolishness that will result in stress and disappointment. Make your intention known, and then trust that all will fall into place. It is pointless fretting. My way is higher than yours, my way considers all, and my way is perfect. We are but one. Your part in creation is proper intention; my part is manifestation. Sometimes what is manifested is beyond anything you could have hoped for. I love you. I delight to give you the desires of your heart if you would but trust me. Trust me, and allow yourself to rest in the knowledge that I care for you.

Appreciate Each Day

Observe life. Notice that everything changes. Children grow, seasons change, and each day is new. Each present moment passes, never to be lived again. Nothing in the world escapes change. Appreciate each moment, knowing it will never come again. Days come and go, seasons change, and people age, but my love for you is always constant. I love you with an unchanging love. My love for you does not depend on your love for me, nor does in depend on what you do. My love for you is all encompassing. It knows no boundaries.

Welcome each day anew, and welcome each moment afresh. Even before you rise up in the morning, be grateful for the new day and for your life. Each morning, attune yourself to your soul and my presence within, and carry that attunement with you throughout the day. Be grateful that you are alive and have a new day in which to live. Each time you interact with a person or any living form, be grateful for its very being.

Maintain A Disposition Of Gratitude

Reflect gratefulness in your everyday living. By learning to be aware and grateful of each moment, you are able to take advantage of opportunities you would have otherwise missed.

Each day is a new day. It has never been lived before. Be attuned to your soul, and listen to the guidance it offers you, for today is different from any other day. Each day offers new opportunities for you. By seizing these opportunities, you are able to increase your capabilities and live this day to your fullest potential. Living in the fullest potential of your being for that day, you are aware of how blessed you are. You are blessed to have awareness, you are blessed to have a body, you are blessed to be alive, and you are blessed to have this day. Treat each day as a new day, and appreciate your life for this day. Each day is a gift given to you. Give yourself afresh to each day.

The sun rises and sets. Every day is a new day, but my love for you remains the same for all eternity. Heed the call of your soul. Know yourself and know me, that I might bless you abundantly. My grace is with you for all time.

Grace

You look within, and when you find your soul, you find love and wisdom. When you find love and wisdom, you find trust and knowledge. All these combined give you an understanding of the fullness of grace. Grace is that feeling that surpasses all others. It is unconditional, accepting love, incomprehensible to your mind, and known only by your spirit. It is grace that pulls you toward truth. It is truth that sets you free to bask in grace. It is through grace that you came into being; it is to grace that you belong. Your soul is inspired by grace. Your soul is tenderly held within grace.

Grace is the expression of my divine nature. It is the highest form of love. Your soul knows grace; it is felt on the soul level rather than in your heart. When you feel grace, your vibration rises. You are aware of a feeling beyond illusion. I am the well of living waters, and your soul is the living water. If anyone is thirsty, let him or her drink from within his or her soul. The well is never ending; the water is always fresh and pure. Your thirst is your quest for truth. Your thirst is satisfied within your own soul, and your quest is answered within.

Look Within

Look within, beyond your mind; look within your soul. It is not hard to find if you genuinely seek.

"Seek ye first the kingdom of heaven, and all these things will be added unto you." This does not mean that you look inside as a means to achieve your other not-so-spiritual goals. It means to make your spirituality your aim, your passion, and your reason for living. Only then does your life begin to make sense, but this is not an objective at all in your quest to know your soul. You seek soul for the purpose of knowing yourself, *not* so that you can become rich. Only with right intention do genuine seekers find what they are looking for. Those who are greedy, selfish, and proud will need to deal with those emotions first before they know their soul.

If they are genuine, they need only ask my spirit to help them, and then they will begin to see the signs pointing them in the right direction. These signs may be in many forms. My spirit is not limited in the methods used. Just be aware and you will see. It is grace that put that desire within you to know your soul and to know me. It is grace that encourages you along the way. It is grace that greets you when you find yourself discovering your soul, for grace lies within your soul within the very depth of your being.

Grace lies within you and around you. As you begin this process, the journey to soul, grace moves to meet you.

Selfish Desires

Little children are of pure intent. They are neither proud nor selfish. In that way, become as a little child and release yourself from selfish desires. Selfish desires are a tool of ego. They act as a curtain hiding your true nature. Your true nature may be hidden, but it is still there. Draw back the curtain of selfish intentions, and expose the light within your own soul. This light is hidden by the curtain of wrong thinking, but behind the curtain, it shines brightly.

It is a wonder that so many of you live in a world of comparative darkness when just the act of clearing the wrong thinking from your minds would illuminate you in liberation. Grace is not forceful. She will not throw back the curtains for you but waits like an anxious parent for you to make that choice. Many of you still battle with the idea that you have a choice. You believe the identity you have created for yourself by your thoughts is the real you. Some are so blinded by ego they do not even question, believing that they are successful in their lives.

What is the purpose to life? Is it to work until you retire and then ponder until you die? Is it to see how much money you can make? Is it to create children and leave a heritage to them? Who were you born to be? When you reflect back on your life, have you lived the life you were meant to live?

The Ultimate Experience

This life is one created by yourself to experience all that you chose to experience and to learn all that you wanted to learn. You came to experience the illusion of separateness. But the ultimate experience and the aim of your life is remembering and reconnecting with your soul. This is the ultimate experience for you and the reason we agreed in the first place to this game of yours.

Sadly, so many now believe this game is real. Oh if I could rouse you, I would. There is no sense in prolonging your suffering life after life. It may seem like a real treadmill to you, but it is an illusion. Many of you have created so much darkness in your lives that you refuse to look within, fearing the darkness is there also, destroying any hope you may have had. If you do not face your soul, you will never know for sure. You will rely on second-hand experiences of others. It is through grace that I give you my blessed assurance that looking within will relieve your fears.

There is no darkness in your soul. Your soul contains your truth. Look into your soul; there is only love. Beloved, if only you could see your own soul, commune with spirit, and accept grace, then the scales would fall from your eyes. You would rejoice as you wake from your dream. The angels in heaven would then have cause for celebration because they would know that you are finally coming home.

Angels

The angels are souls who chose not to experience the illusion of separateness. They have not been subject to wrong thinking resulting in suffering, but they are very aware of the paths you are each on.

Some of you have had experiences with angels in your lives. They come to surround you with hope, and they hover in the background of your lives like a silent witness who is there to support you if asked. Angels are divine messengers sent by me to guide you when you wish to be guided. Often the angels will protect you from some misadventure or calamity that would impact your life negatively. They will intervene if something will take you too far from your chosen path.

CHAPTER 13

The End Of Fear

No Condemnation

Love and grace await you when you decide to choose union over separateness. There is no condemnation or judgment over things you have done or haven't done. As you remember it is all an illusion or a dream, whatever happens in your dream does not affect reality because it was never real. What you do, think, or feel have consequences only in your dream. It is important that you understand this truth: you are not judged in spirit for errors committed in your lives as humans. Wrong thinking or actions do affect you because while these exist in your life, you are held back from soul as dark and light do not exist together. Therefore, if you leave your mortal body, you will need to continue the game in another body until you break free from illusion by recognising your wrong thinking and revealing your truth.

In other words, the game is not over for you until the objective has been met. The objective is to know yourself as soul; to recognise yourself as a part of me with everything that means; and to reconcile with the light of spirit. I urge you to consider your original purpose for being and seek it as you would a great treasure. I urge you to consider this in this lifetime because once you live your purpose; you can wake up at home and will be spared anymore of your bad dream. Remember, there is no condemnation on your return to me because I am love and grace. Condemnation, being of the dark, cannot exist in my light. There will be rejoicing and celebration because you are my beloved and I long for you to recognise our holy communion. Our holy communion, our oneness, exists, but not in your mind. That does not mean it is not real. It means you are dreaming and have yet to waken.

You Are Free

Decide to see the good in others and you will recognise the good in yourself, for their spirit is the same as yours. You see your reflection through spirit. As you move from being unaware to aware, unconscious to conscious, you are able to wake others by shining your light from within your heart into theirs. You consciously co-create your life, and you are able to separate the truth from the illusion. All the time you are aware that it is by grace that you are free. You are free because you accepted that you are blameless, as was Christ. You are free because knowing yourself, you know that you are within my spirit, united with all life, but you are also an individual soul. Likewise, all of nature is designed to represent the holy relationship. Each snowflake is unique but still part of the snowfall.

Your soul is unique to you, but you are one with spirit. Every living organism contains spirit. It is the life force that flows through them. In that way you are all part of my spirit, for my spirit is the life force of all. My spirit contains all life. Nothing that lives is void of spirit. In this way, you are one with the all, just as the snowflake is one with the snow. From the depths of your being, your soul has access to all knowledge. As this knowledge appears to you, you have no need to prove it is correct, for you feel it to be truth; you *know* it. A truth of spirit when revealed is truth remembered. As soul, you know the spiritual truths. They are ingrained in you, for as soul you are that truth. You are divine truth. There is nothing false in truth, and there is no darkness in your light.

Obstacles

Obstacles arise on your spiritual quest, which at first seem like stumbling blocks, but as you move toward the light, the light shines on the stumbling blocks. When you become aware of them, you then use them as stepping stones. Negative emotions appear as stumbling blocks, but the closer to the light you are, the more the light of love shines on them through your awareness, changing them to stepping stones as you learn to control them through love.

Cessation Of Fear

I did not create fear. You created fear in your mind. It is not real, for your mind is the only place it exists. Your mind, when it is separated from me, is false, just as you are false when you are separated from me.

Shining the light of love on fear is just like exposing a camera's film to the light. It becomes void of pictures, as the pictures of fear in your mind cease to exist under exposure to light and love.

Fear is part of the illusion. In reality it does not exist. Choose love as a way of looking at a situation rather than viewing it through fear. Fear is only a wall created by your ego to shield you from your full power. Fear is a symptom of separation. Although the basis of fear is not real, the reactions it causes within your body are. The perceived fear triggers a chain of reaction that is felt in the physical body and then vibrated into your very essence through different layers of your being. This becomes embedded in your etheric body, resulting in feelings of being out of balance or just not being in optimum health. These scars in your etheric body can be healed through spiritual healing or by yourself reconciling to soul. All negative feelings stem from fear. Greed, envy, pride, and even sorrow all originally come from fear. When you're sad, you are afraid that the dream you are living is real. Believing that all living entities are eternal and waking up to find that true for you dissolves the fear and in turn the sadness.

Turn Darkness Into Light

My love for you is all encompassing. In that way, I would hasten your recognition of your true nature so your illusion is shattered and you fear no more. Begin the process of waking up by proving to yourself there is no fear and no validity in any negative emotion except that you may learn from it to turn your darkness into light. In any instance where a negative feeling arises in you, trace it back to its very roots, shine the light of love upon those roots, and watch it disintegrate. In that way you will begin to dissolve your own illusion and know what I say to be true.

Grace will fill your heart with her truth and encourage you to follow the truth of your being. In that way, you find your soul. All negative emotions come from false thinking created by your own mind. As you begin the process of waking up, you grow into your real power within, and you learn from your soul how to control your mind.

Thoughts Are Tools

Your thoughts are but tools of your mind. Your mind chooses the tools for its use. Your mind may be controlled by ego or by soul. Your mind has a choice to choose negative or positive thoughts. These thoughts then decide your feelings, which, as you now know, influence your life for better or for worse because they can attract or repel manifestations in your life. Learning to use your mind as a bridge between the invisible and the visible can either increase the illusion or cement your roots in soul again; it is your choice.

Role of Ego

Your ego is the part of you that was so necessary for your creation in this realm. If it was not for ego, you would not be experiencing all that you are. The ego's purpose was to keep you from the reward of truth until you learned and experienced all you chose to do before you took the form you are now in. The ego is the jailer of your soul, guarding it from truth until the holy instant when the captive soul is released to freedom. The will of ego then becomes one with the will of your soul, which is one with mine. Your will, which you may have considered to be isolated and small, you now know to be in union with mine. This knowledge gives you the confidence to go forth in grace toward any goal you made in spirit. You are aware of your soul's purpose and move confidently in the direction that you must go to achieve this.

The alignment of ego and soul results in harmony of spirit. This harmony is reflected back down through the etheric layers of your body and results in a feeling of well-being or all being well within your soul.

CHAPTER 14

The Presence Of The Divine

My Presence Is In The Present

You Are In Me And I *Am* In You

Standing Within Me, You Have No Limits

Change Pain Into Happiness

You Cannot Fail At Being You

Power

Stand Tall

My Presence Is In The Present

Time is not a factor when you flow within spirit because the present moment is all there is. My presence is in the present. If you are consciously aware of spirit in that moment, then you instinctively know that time is nothing to be concerned over because everything that needs to happen, happens. Then you can rest in the peace that aligning with spirit brings, and you find that worry faded with your old nature.

Your old nature had a small, limited view of life; your new nature sees a life without the limits imposed by fear and freedom to be your true self, as spirit is free. No longer do you have a need to look outside of yourself to satisfy ego, but you look within to satisfy soul and know that you are God.

You are one with me.

You Are In Me And I *Am* In You

You are a part of me, but you contain my essence. In me you live, move, and have your being. In you; I *am*. You live for me, with me, and in me because of me. You are here; you are there, knowing yourself to be more than your body. In me, you can be you; in you, I *am*. Separation, being only an illusion, no longer exists. You are me; your hands and your voice are a vehicle of spirit. My spirit and your spirit are the same; we are one. Moving in your holy power, you help the waking of mankind. The light extends, and the darkness must then contract. Your reality is determined by your awareness that physical, mental, and emotional states not only exist concurrently but also exist within different frequencies. Your reality is your vibration.

Standing Within Me, You Have No Limits

Awake in the moment, you are consciously aware that you still have the choice of your thoughts. You consistently notice that they are compatible with your state of grace. If for any reason you feel incompatible with the state of grace, you find you can alter your thoughts and choices accordingly, and this becomes natural for you.

In me you are always at peace, regardless of external circumstances. Keep attuned to me by being aware of your feelings.

In this way you change yourself to be who you want to be through grace because you cannot be in your fullness of being by retaining limited, negative thoughts. These negative, limiting thoughts have no power unless you accommodate them, for then they, being vibrations of energy, will affect your physical reality. Retain conscious control over your mind. As you do, your understanding and respect for yourself grow. In this way you have attained higher thought and peace and act within spirit. No other living being can take this sense of inner empowerment from you unless you let them by lowering your level of thought. Always identify with your holy power, and you will sense any negativity as a drain in your energy as it leaks this from you.

No longer will you let things affect you, but moving in spirit, guided by soul, *you* will affect your environment by your thoughts.

Opinions and criticisms from others no longer find their mark with you, for you walk confidently in faith, strong in the knowledge of yourself.

Change Pain Into Happiness

You are a co-creator with me. You no longer react to your environment. You see it only as the manifestation of your past thoughts and instead you find your environment responding to you. You are able to walk away from illusion, just like walking out from under an umbrella into the sunshine. There are no barriers now for you, only those that persist in your mind. My beloved, know that the pain you once created from your own ignorance you can change into happiness by your own awareness. Let the light from your soul guide you, and listen carefully to the still, small voice within. Recognise that voice as my voice as I share with you things that are beyond the understanding of your old nature.

As the light of your soul dawns on your life, you can look back at the night, knowing it was but a dream and look forward with hope and love. What you want is no longer based in selfish desire because truth and wisdom give you the power and freedom to control your destiny through love. Controlling your destiny in this way is within my divine will for your soul because I only want the best for you, and you are very capable of living this life to your fullest potential.

You were born to be the greatest you that you can be.

Do not doubt yourself, and do not belittle yourself. Move forward in boldness; the world needs you.

You Cannot Fail At Being You

Oh my sweetest child, there is only one of you. Be great within yourself, you cannot fail at being you, so follow your soul's calling and be the you that you were meant to be. Your life is what you want it to be; it is the reality of your dreams. Your life is hard if you want it that way; it is easy if you want it that way. I know that you may say your life is hard and you do not want it that way, but now it is revealed to you that your thoughts have sculpted your reality, so if you want a better life, then do not continue to see your life as hard.

By choosing to continue to see your life as hard, you are choosing not to see your life as easy. It is in that way that, if your life is hard, it is because you want it that way because you have chosen to see it that way, and so you thereby create its reality.

Your life matches what you believe yourself to be.

Some of the lessons you have chosen to learn on this journey may be difficult, but their ultimate lesson was to learn grace. I am grace, and in me you step into grace without any need for further lessons. Your beliefs define where you are in life. If you believe yourself to be unworthy of happiness, you will create the thoughts to bind yourself to your belief.

Your beliefs are separate from you. If you change your belief and believe that you are worthy of happiness, your thoughts will change accordingly. You are separate from your beliefs. Imagine how you would like your life to be, and then construe the beliefs you would need to support that reality. By faith in those beliefs, your thoughts will change accordingly, and by grace your new reality will manifest.

Power

You are powerful; you are strong in your true being. This inherent power within you is your own nature. Your own true being has no fear. It is bold in its identity.

If you know yourself, you know me. I am in you, and you are in me. The knowledge of this working relationship is power.

Many of you are not moving in your power. You are not moving in your power because you fail to recognise it as part of your being. You may believe others have power over you or that you have given your power away.

Oh sweet child, nobody is more powerful than you, and you cannot possibly give part of your being away. It is only a mistaken belief. You are all spirit beings all with equal power. It is only what you choose to believe that differs. Take a grasp of yourself and of your situation. Do you believe you are powerless in any instance? Change your belief. Believe that you have claimed your rightful power and nobody or no situation can deny you that. You are strong, and you are powerful. Realising this truth sets you free from believing yourself to be less.

Knowing yourself, you know yourself in me, and your understanding of that truth liberates your spirit. Stand tall. You are no longer a victim of life's circumstances. Stand tall, take your rightful place, know that you belong, know that you have a true path, and know that you are *always* safe.

Stand Tall

Stand tall, and take responsibility for your own life. Take charge and master your life in the way of your soul.

You are safe in me from the dangers you would create with your own mind. It is never too late to change your beliefs. It is never too late to claim your power. It is never too late to change the course of your life and to live your true path in boldness. Later, as you reflect on your life, you will be glad you took the stand rather than regretting what you did not do. By claiming your power, you are really just claiming your you-ness. Be confident, and walk tall. You are important to the world. Be confident, and walk tall; you are important to me. Know your place. As you go forth along your true path, know that nothing can stop you on your purpose.

Believe in yourself and in your strength and all that means for you.

CHAPTER 15

The Answer Is Within

Reason

Richness

Choice

Faith

Give Of Yourself

We Are One

Tap In

Reason

You are where you are for a reason. You have experienced all that you have for a reason. Nothing is random. Everything has meaning. You are here for a reason, but you cannot use reason to find it. Look within. *You are the reason.* The reason you are here is you. Know yourself.

Richness

You are able to appreciate the richness of your being as you feel complete in your true nature. You have satisfaction and freedom within your being. As you witness this, you have abundant life. This is abundant living. You want for nothing, and you need nothing to give you the satisfaction and freedom that is already yours. You are content with all that you have *within* even though externally you may appear to have little. There are those who have so much externally and still require more in the hope that they will achieve real satisfaction and freedom. Having lots of assets and desiring more, they are still empty within.

You who have inner contentment do not need anything else to give you freedom and satisfaction. In this way you are rich. You have abundance of peace, freedom, satisfaction, and contentment. Your life is so full with the goodness of spirit, and because it is continually flowing, it overflows from you to others, for what good is the overflow if it has nowhere to go? You are my beloved, and the overflow from your life is like an overflow of me because I *am* in you. Spread your truth and your light. Relax in the knowledge that all your needs are taken care of as you turn first to me. You are rich in all that you have and in all that you give.

Choice

There are always choices to be made. Your choices determine your reality. All of your choices are based on the knowledge available to you at that instant. Knowledge comes from what you believe according to your perceptions. It is what your mind perceives that determines your reality. As you integrate this knowledge into your being, you come to an understanding of it.

My beloved, choose to open your heart and your mind to know your soul. By choosing to know your soul, you choose to know me. Oh that you would know your true being and live your life to the full in the company of your soul. I love you.

Water poured freely on the ground can only benefit a plant if it passes through layers of dirt in order to reach the roots. Likewise, my spirit is all around, but if it cannot enter your awareness, you cannot benefit from me. Just as water is to the plant, my spirit is to you.

You make choices based on what you believe to be true according to your perceptions. You cannot perceive me within the capabilities of your senses. You cannot force my spirit to fit your beliefs. Therefore, accepting me as a truth that cannot be perceived, a mystery that cannot be explained, requires faith. The faith of a little child is all the faith you need, for it is on accepting this belief without proof that you gain understanding. It is your choice to move in faith because understanding me lies beyond belief.

Faith

Faith is the substance of things hoped for and the evidence that things exist, although as yet they are not perceived by the senses. This faith is to be unwavering, without doubt, for presence of doubt nullifies faith. Indecision is the presence of doubt. For anything you ask for, in faith believe and you will receive. In this way, imagine what you want and match your beliefs to it as if by faith you already have it. Ask (release it) and you will receive it. Give thanks for it before you receive it, and after it materialises, in this way your connection to spirit remains strong. You gratitude for things received in your spirit but not yet perceived by your senses is faith. If you have the faith of a mustard seed, you can move mountains. As long as you acknowledge spirit, the illusion of separatism remains as a dream. There is no benefit in returning to the darkness. Jesus came into the world as light and declared that whoever believed in him should not remain in the darkness. You share the same spirit as Jesus. By believing in him or believing in your true nature, you bring the light into your life, leaving the darkness of your dream.

Give Of Yourself

It is not so much about what you receive or how much you attract. Your life is about how much you give. Give of yourself. As you progress in our holy relationship, you become aware of love growing within you for the whole of mankind, but what good is this love if it is not active? Act on the compassion you feel for others. Give out your light to them. If you are able to help another in need, do so with gladness in your heart. Do not turn your back on those in dire circumstances, for in other instances, your roles may be reversed. Freely give, expecting nothing in return.

Some of you are self-absorbed on your spiritual journey to the extent that you forget this journey is one to be shared and there are those who are still feeling alone and separate. Reach out your hand where you can, and share your message of grace. The very act of helping someone remove the scales from his or her eyes is above all cost. You cannot put a value on helping to set them free.

We Are One

Trust in me; know that you are not in this life on your own, for I, the almighty, reside within you. We are one, but some of you have yet to recognise that. Often you search for information in books, but there comes a time when you no longer need to read to learn because you "just know." By looking elsewhere other than within, you still only see me as a part of life somewhere out there. This implies that I am separate from you. Is it any wonder so many of you feel incomplete?

If you gaze at the stars looking for infinity, you are aware of where you are standing. Likewise, as you observe the intricacy of a leaf, you are aware it is just a leaf. When you look within yourself, there is only awareness. You are awareness, you are never-ending, infinite love, and this is your true nature. Your mind is a part of my divine mind. My mind inspires yours; you contain all the information necessary for inspired living. Look within, and tap in.

Tap In

Tap into my wisdom within you. As you acknowledge that you are one with me, you surrender to the all and you gain the all. In fact, the battle to retain your individual power was a battle only in your fearful mind. In choosing love, there is no battle, only a sweet melting into your true self. There were times before you aligned your will with mine when I would gently nudge you in order to redirect you from needless pain. Those of you who ignored the nudge suffered the pain. Know that when I nudge, I have your best interests at heart. I love you. I love you, you are my creation, and each one of you is loved beyond measure. You have freedom of will; my will for you is that you share in glory with me and in making your will one with mine. All I have is yours. Oh that I would bless you. My kingdom is within you. All those who enter in discover the riches that have been laid up for them. My kingdom is within you. It is within your very soul. Open yourself, for the keys to my kingdom are in your mind. The power and the glory are eternally yours as you turn the key of your thoughts inward to your soul.

CHAPTER 16

The Importance Of Each Being

Our Voice

My kingdom is within you. As your will becomes one with mine, the voice you hear from your soul is our voice. Learn to listen to this voice. Your soul speaks from wisdom—my wisdom. It is so. I, the God of all creation, speak to you from love, by grace through your own soul. In this way, we communicate and commune together. The words resonating in your soul are audible in your heart. You hear my words. In turn, the words you speak are powerful. They come from your thoughts and are manifested into form. It is a way of commanding your thoughts. Those of you who hear my voice can speak my words to those yet in darkness. In that way, you are my voice. You are the voice of my truth.

My beloved, remember the voice of truth because it helps them to recognise the very same voice within their souls. My voice is one voice but with many messages that can be heard in all souls at any one time. I speak through soul by my spirit to all who would hear. Listen to your soul. Its truths are birthed in me, and the words you hear are intended for your highest good.

Commune with me; commune with your soul.

The Word

Jesus is my Word. In him I dwell. Every cell of his being is attuned to me. In that way, his every thought, deed, and spoken word is from me, as is his being in me and me in him. I am in you, and you are in me, but many are not yet aware of this, and of those who are, most do not realise the full magnitude of this glorious communion. Jesus is the way, the truth, and the life.

The *way* to what? The truth.

The *truth* about what? The life.

Whose *life*? Yours.

Jesus is my light made manifest. He embodied the way. The only way to know me is to know the truth about your life. Know yourself.

Walk in the light by the way he taught. The kingdom of heaven is within. The only way to me is knowing yourself because you cannot know the truth without knowing me, for you are a part of me. By knowing yourself, you identify with me.

Your word is powerful because sound is energy. Your words bring life, joy, and understanding to others. Communication is power. One feels the impact of spoken words more readily than a word unspoken. The deaf read lips, not minds. Nobody can read thoughts. Your voice is a spoken thought. By walking in the light, you show the way for others through your truth about your life and your being.

Emotion

Emotion is the catalyst that creates manifestation. That is why you can read something or see something that causes you to think, but without emotion, thoughts do not manifest. In that way, not all thoughts are manifested. Thoughts without focus, emotion, and intent have so little power to manifest that their energy is used in other ways. Thoughts are manifested according to the belief that they will come into being. According to your faith, let it be so. Sometimes just as it takes a long time for an acorn to grow to an oak tree, so too is there a seemingly long time delay between when you send out a thought with intent and its manifestation.

Some things are manifested instantaneously, and other things take time. All of you are co-creators. Many of you are unaware of the power within your mind, but awareness is not in the equation to manifest. Just as surely, I abide in each of you, whether you are aware of my presence or not. It matters not that you are aware, because it is so. Having the power to manifest innately within you, your awareness is reflected in how you choose to think. Being consciously aware of your thoughts and choosing only those that arise from goodness ensures alignment with your purpose. Know that you create without limit because you are within me, and within me there are no limits.

Purpose

Each of you has a purpose, your soul's agenda. Each and every one of you has a purpose. Even those who are severely handicapped from birth and those who are brain damaged and may even appear to have no mind have a purpose. Their souls are like the largest tree in the forest. They are just being. All their soul wanted was just to be. They are just as precious as you because everyone is one in spirit. Now let them just be, and love them for it.

You are all love. Nobody is a burden. You are all teachers.

If you are attuned to your spirit and your life is flowing, that is good. If it appears that something is not right, and if you feel you are swimming against the tide, consider listening within to your soul. If you feel that you are travelling in the wrong direction, you are able to do a U-turn at any time and take the exit that says, "Right Way." It is when your soul is at peace that you are in alignment with its agenda for your life. You are innately spiritual beings. You came from spirit, and you will return to spirit. Do not try to deny who you really are. Your truth is who you are. You do not have an identity crisis. When you wonder who you are, you have a spiritual block. Remove the block, and give yourself the freedom to be you. Look within to find yourself. Do not wonder what you would like to do with your life until you know who you are. So many keep themselves busy doing this or that. They never feel totally settled. How can they when it is only their ego that is content? Their soul cries to be revealed as their true nature. When they deny their souls, they deny their true path.

Pieces Of The Puzzle

Some of you are at a stage where you feel you should be doing something but are not sure what that is. To you I say, consider a caterpillar. When it is time for it to turn into a chrysalis, it just knows what to do, and when it is time for you to need to do something, you will know too.

Sometimes you are led to do things that are in preparation for your purpose. This learning or cleansing experience that you may go through is necessary for your higher good or your purpose. You will be able to reflect and see how it all fits together like a jigsaw puzzle. It is hard to see the whole picture when you have only a few pieces. Like a puzzle, when you intend to complete the picture, you follow the call of your soul until you understand the basic outline, and then the pieces fall into place easily. Often there is a tendency to just cruise through life, experiencing this and that. It is only when you get enough of the pieces that your life makes any sense.

Once you get a glimpse of the goal, your purpose is defined and you move toward it boldly, knowing that this is your reason for living. Do not stop at one piece of the puzzle, do not stop halfway, and do not stop following the voice of your soul until it leads you to your very meaning for your life. Do not give in or give up. If you are feeling that there is something you need to be doing with your life—there is. If you are feeling as though something is missing in your life, find it. If you feel that I am prompting you through your soul, heed it. You all are capable of creating your life by your thoughts, but unless it matches with your soul's purpose, you will never be satisfied with your life because you are not reaching your full potential.

You Are Unique

You are all unique. All of you are a part of the oneness of my spirit, but you are all unique souls. There is not one other soul who could possibly meet your divine agenda but you. Look at your body. Could an eye be a lung? Could a hair be a toe? Each part has its part, as it is with you. Individual parts make up the one. The parts to your body all contain the same DNA found throughout the whole body. The parts of my spirit all contain the same spirit. Just as a body needs each of its parts, I need each of you. In me you dwell, and just like the parts of your physical body, each of you has your own special purpose. It just would not work if a single hair tried to be a toe. In the same way, your life does not work if you are trying to be something that you are not. Be true to your soul because that is the very nature of your being. Within your soul lies your purpose. Do not go against the grain. Do not swim against the current. Go with the flow, and the peace of your soul will show you the way.

Listen to the call of your heart, attend the prompting of your soul, and nurture your spirit. Without a doubt, you are all made of energy. Without a doubt, you each have access to your soul and the truths it contains therein. You are spiritual, eternal beings.

CHAPTER 17

The Oneness Of All

The Play Of Life

Peace Within

Burdens

The Process Of Life Is A Continuous Flow

The Play Of Life

Each of you is loved beyond measure regardless of your part in the play of life. Think of life as a play. Some of the actors have main parts and some have smaller parts, but the play needs everybody for its production. Everybody has value. The actors in the play are so caught up with their roles that they forget it is a play. It becomes very real for them. It is only when the play is over that they stop acting and become real. In this way, when you step out of the play of life, you realise another perspective. There are those among you who do not realise that they are in the play until their costume (body) is removed (death).

Your soul is infinite in power and love. It cannot be contained in a body, but it can be found within your body. As within, so without. Know your soul as yourself. Look within and understand all.

You are precious vessels containing your individual soul. Do not deny its existence, for then you would be nothing but a void. My love, your soul is the treasure within you. You do not have to seek as such; just look within. You are beautiful; you are fashioned out of a part of me. The part of me that resides in you is creative, playful, and powerful. This is your divine nature. When you use your divine nature, you no longer need negative thinking or negative emotions. Despair, worry, and anger you left behind with your old, egotistical nature. Your divine nature contains your full potential. Develop your positive attitude, look for synchronicities, and show your light to the world. Feel the love and joy, because your soul brings your reward of internal peace.

Peace Within

It is this internal peace that eludes so many who search for it in the wrong places. It is this internal peace that is the peace that surpasses all understanding. This internal peace is an indicator that all is well within your soul. This internal peace is eternal peace. There is nothing in your world that could compare with the peace of spirit. This peace is the soul basking in the delight of spirit. I am a God of love and a God of peace. Mountains and hills may crumble, but my love for you will never crumble. All those who commune with me are promised my peace because they are forever blessed. In all decisions, you are faced with a choice. The right choice is the one that gives you peace. In all your life, live according to the peace of your soul. By this peace you will know my will for your life. Even when the world around you may seem to be chaotic, your inner peace remains unshaken. Look within and feel your soul. My ways are higher than yours, my thoughts are higher than yours, and my grace is all encompassing. As you abide in the realm of spirit, I delight to give you the desires of your heart. Even though you may not yet perceive it, have faith, for all will be revealed. By following the peace within your soul, you follow the path of your greatest good.

Your peace is a testament to my guidance for you, for if you follow the peace that reigns in your soul, you follow me.

Burdens

And truly I say to you, I will pour my blessings upon all those who follow me and make their burden light. The burden you carry is symbolic of issues that you are attached to. When you lose your attachment to these issues, they either disappear or are changed into an aspect of your purpose. Either way, when you shine the light of love onto the burden, it is shown as to what it really is. If the burden is related to your purpose, the reason that is so will become clear.

Some of you may carry a burden for a while in your life, just as a physical weight that you carry, it can make you strong or it can make you bend.

For some of you a heavy burden is used by spirit to be a cause of discomfort because it is only when the burden gets so heavy that you search your mind for a way to rid yourself of such a heavy weight. Beyond resolve, you have no options left, so in desperation you look within to your soul, which leads you to rest in the lightness of spirit, for my peace is your peace; to be a bearer of the light is not heavy. Allow me to carry your burden so you can be that clear channel. Direct all worries through to me, and in turn, let my love and wisdom flow through you without question. Do not hold sorrows, worries, or fears because these act as a block in your channel and hinder the flow coming from me via your soul. Release all burdens to me. Let go of them completely so your ego no longer interferes with all its negativity. Trust that the best outcome for soul is what I give.

Live in the present, and go with the flow of spirit.

The Process Of Life Is In A Continuous Flow

You cannot separate yourself from the process of life. By going with the flow and acknowledging that indeed you are a part of life, you discover the feeling of oneness. In that oneness, you know me beyond defining. Nothing in your limited reality can define me. I am infinite space, and all matter exists in me.

It is only when your reality becomes one with mine that you are unlimited and know me beyond defining.

Your soul always seeks the divine path for your life. Let it lead you. Live according to soul. Do not worry over the past or the future, as then you will not experience this present moment. My presence is in the present. The future is always ahead of you. You can never live it now. Live only now. Live today by the flow of your soul, knowing that all is well, and trust me to unfold all your tomorrows, which will be so much better than you could have ever planned.

Life is a process. You cannot go with the flow if you are attached to things. The people who are meant to be in your life catch the same wave and you flow together.

Do not bind yourself with a false sense of security in things. Be prepared to go with the flow. There will be times when you rest in the rock-pools of the stream of life, but then, when it is time to move on, your soul will let you know. Learn to trust in the process of life.

CHAPTER 18

The Gift Of Self

Gifts

Appreciate Your Gifts

Do Not Hide Your Talents

No Gift Is Inferior

Healing

Gifts

Many of you have gifts and talents, but unless you are using them in line with your soul's purpose, you are limiting them. Allow me to use your gifts and talents through you. I need clear channels through which to work. Become that blank canvas, and let the artist within your soul speak. Your conscious mind only perceives with your senses, and from that perception, understanding arises. The understanding received by your conscious mind is limited as your senses are limited in their perception. It is only with your spiritual mind, your higher state of consciousness, that you can perceive from beyond your self-imposed boundaries. These perceptions are often in the form of inspiration. Inspiration is sourced in me. It is only by stilling your mind that you are able to channel my thoughts. My thoughts come from all that is. Inspiration enhances the talent you already have, enabling you to become brilliant in how you apply yourself. Everyone is capable of reaching his or her full potential. Everyone is capable of listening within.

Appreciate Your Gifts

Trust yourself; trust me. Trust the guidance of your soul. Acknowledge your gifts and appreciate them. In all things be thankful, and in all things be humble. Acknowledge the source of your gift and to you more will be given. Gifts that I give are meant to be shared, because by giving to one, all benefit. All gifts from me bring joy and love to the hearts of those who receive them. All gifts from me resonate with truth. I am a generous giver, and you are my beloved children. I delight in giving to you. Many of you received these gifts before you were even born. These gifts lay dormant in you until the time was right for you to discover them. It was only fitting in some instances that you grew into them. If you discovered them earlier, you could not have done them justice. It is only when you use your gifts for their divine purpose that you are able to grasp the realisation of their meaning.

I am the giver of perfect gifts that are personally designed for each recipient. However, some of you, feeling yourself to be unworthy, even though aware of your gift are too scared to make use of it. You are all worthy, and your gift will bring you pleasure. Do not deny my giving. Do not deny others the pleasure of benefiting from your gift; do not deny yourself the joy of sharing. You are worthy of my gifts, and the talents you have are meant to be shared. Do not worry that they will not be received, for I tell you that doors will be opened and your skills welcomed. The way is already prepared for those desiring to use their gifts to further my kingdom. I do not give gifts that are of no use.

Do Not Hide Your Talents

The world needs and wants what you have to share. Step out in faith; do not hide your talent. I do not need you to be timid in who you are but to be bold. Be bold in my strength, and go forth. If you are faced with uncertainty about where or how to use your gifts to ensure their utmost potential, listen within to your soul. Some doors will close while others will open, and there will be synchronicity as you and your gift flow with spirit. Learn to be aware of the signs pointing in the direction you must go.

Be alert, and be awake. It is for your higher good that you walk on the divine path for your life. It is for your higher good that you share your talents with those ready to receive them. Please do not doubt yourself; you were given these talents for a reason. That reason was for you to enjoy them. They are yours. They feel natural. Use them to benefit other souls. Also encourage others to take full advantage of their gifts. By enjoying your talents and using them, you inspire others to begin to use theirs.

The greatest of all gifts you received was the ability to be yourself.

No Gift Is Inferior

You are unique and precious, and using the gift of being yourself requires that you be the best you that you can be. In being the best that you can be, you are naturally you. By looking within this natural you, you discover your strengths. Even your soft-heartedness, which you saw as a weakness, may be revealed to be a strong gift. My ways are different from yours. Nobody can fail at being themselves. It may be that your personality is your inherent gift. Take all your talents and skills and use them; never be ashamed or embarrassed. All your gifts are valuable. Each one is suited to each unique individual. If you feel that you have been given an inferior gift, you are denying yourself the opportunity to discover its richness. No gift is inferior. All are given in love, to be used in love.

Enjoy your talents; I did not make a mistake giving them to you. Use them for your higher good and the higher good of others. It is the nature of some gifts to expand as you accept them and use them. In this way, people with a gift of singing who are attuned to their spirits will find their voices grow with them as they grow in their stature of souls. Learn to be grateful for what you have received, trusting in my love for you. My love for you is interwoven in your gifts. All gifts are given in love. My love for you is so great that many are happy just to accept that. But I tell you that as sure as my love is for you; each of you has strengths and talents. They were not given to you to be unused. Use your talents and strengths to bless others and yourself. Your being, your very soul, is so very precious to me. I am sensitive to everything about you. You may feel you are very ordinary, but to me you are all extraordinary, each with your own special purpose. You are one of a kind. All that I create has purpose, and all that I create is good.

Healing

I gave you the power to heal yourself, as Jesus demonstrated on others, but so many of you look elsewhere for your healing. There are some who specialise in healing in the way of spirit, but once you are free of illusion, you are able to heal yourself and others through faith.

Draw my healing energy down through your very being, and with your hands or your thoughts, direct this energy where you want it to go. In this way you can heal animals also. I am love. In me there is no sickness, so draw my energy through yourself. Sickness cannot live in my energy. As you direct my energy with your thoughts, you are able to direct healing even over a distance to people and animals. My energy through you passes in through their energy layers, transforming negative energy and balancing their energy system. Sometimes it is only the balancing of their energy systems that is required.

Some of you claim the healing energies as your own, denying their source. This is fine for those still under the illusion of separateness, as any energy directed with the intent of healing is good. However, by believing yourself to be separate, you limit the amount of energy you use. When you wake to the light, you are able to use the energy of *all*.

Beloved child, do not think I have forsaken you in your sickness. Look within. You contain my holy spirit, and you have the power to heal yourself. Listen within. The voice of truth you hear is mine residing in your soul. Listen and heed. You have the power to heal yourself within. Rise above doubt and heal yourself.

CHAPTER 19

The Illusion Of Darkness

Sickness

Disease By Choice

Demons

Walk In The Light

Darkness Is An Illusion

Sickness

Those of you who are inflicted with sickness know that it is not of me. Unless you chose to be born with it, it is rooted in wrong thinking and wrong feeling.

Any person who finds the truth is one with me, and there is no sickness within me.

Wrong eating can cause sickness, but this comes also from wrong thinking. Those who follow the light become pure in thought; by loving themselves, they know what their bodies need to be healthy. They only partake of foods and drinks that are agreeable to their bodies. Do not believe that I would test you by afflicting you with some disease. I only want good things for you, for I am a God of goodness and light. Darkness and ill health cannot abide in me.

If you are sick, look into your soul and find the cause of your sickness. When you find the cause, shine the light of love upon it until it disappears. Then my spirit will renew your strength, and you will mount up as an eagle. If the cause of your sickness evades you, ask that it be shown to you, and wait patiently for that still, small voice within to reveal the answer.

Disease By Choice

Negative energy from wrong thinking can manifest as disease. Dis-ease exists in those who are not at ease. Be at ease within yourself, and allow spirit to flow through you, ridding yourself of any negativity that may exist as blockages in your energy system. Peace in your body, mind, and spirit indicates all is well in your soul.

Regardless of how sick a body is, the soul is always in full health.

There are those who have chosen to either experience illness or to be born with disease or deformity. These are souls who have come to be loved and often inspire others to use their gifts that have lain dormant within them.

Demons

The only demons that possess a sick person are the demons of wrong thought or wrong emotion. Demons are not entities that have entered into people. Jesus himself was accused of having demons within him, and you too may be accused of inviting evil. As you move into your authentic power, the demon of fear will try to stop you. This demon of fear is the fear of exposure because when the light of your truth and love hit it, it lives no more. Can you not see that simply by believing in demons, your mere belief creates them in your mind? Is it any wonder, then, that they are easy to deal with?

By believing in the light or using the name synonymous with the light, Jesus, demons have to flee, because darkness cannot exist in the light. Where there is light, there are no demons. Therefore if people believe they have a demon, they have one according to their belief because they have created it out of fear. Even as they direct their thoughts elsewhere, their demon disappears. As you shine your light and speak your truth, the demon will disperse. Protect yourself from negative energies by walking in the light. Negative energies only exist as long as the idea of separatism exists. When the illusion is shattered, all negative energy is transmuted into goodness under the process of grace.

Walk In The Light

All those who walk in the light are protected by the light. When you face the light of truth, the shadows of fear disappear in much the same way that your shadow disappears when you face the sun. When darkness seems to be all around you, remember the light you hold within. Walk in the light. Often the light is just on the other side of your fear. Have confidence and know for certain that if you really look at your fear, you will find the light. I know that for some to ignore or run from their pain, anger or fear is the preferred option. I *am* truth, and I say to you that there is no fear, anger, or pain that can exist when you look through it to the light. I *am* the light. There is no fear, anger, or pain in me.

The Light

Using your authentic power and working from soul, you become as light. This light is a beacon of truth to others. There are those who profess to be of the light, but in boasting of their powers, they push themselves forward, shining only a reflection of their ego selves. This reflection may be regarded as a shield because it may mislead the seekers who, in their great hunger, may believe they have caught a glimpse of the light. If you have the intention to help others, help yourself first. Then in knowing the light, you become the light. Your reflection is then the truth of your being.

It is only by knowing yourself completely as part of me that you realise you are a part of the flow of life. Everything in your reality is interrelated. Seeing yourself as isolated is a false perception of your ego consciousness. Therefore, loving your neighbour is the same as loving yourself. There is only oneness, and this oneness is light. It is just those who sleep who have their eyes closed to it, for in me there is no darkness, and I am all there is.

Darkness Is An Illusion

Darkness is but an illusion you have created to subjectively feel the light.

You created the darkness in order to dream. In your dream, you forgot who you were, but on waking to the light, you remember and reclaim your true nature. Your true nature is within my essence; my essence is your true nature. You are light. Your life is a wave of light within a never-ending ocean of light, constantly flowing in the current of oneness. Understand that you are supported in light, and you are supported by my love. You are all in the light, although some do not know it yet because they are still sleeping.

Regardless of your awareness of the light, you all abide in it because you all abide in me. There is no escaping because that is all that there is. There is no escaping from the all because you are a part of the all. My love for you is unchanging; it supports you both in form and out of form, both as a physical being and a spiritual being. My love for you is always present. You are never alone, even in your darkest moments. You are never alone, for I am always in you. Any time you are lonely, look within. Grace will lead you to your soul. When you find and know your soul, you recognise yourself, and you recognise me.

You are my beloved. I love you dearly. Open your eyes, my child. It is time to wake up. Remember me; I have never forgotten you. I *am* with you always. Even in infinity, I *am* there with you. You are infinity. Beyond time and space, you exist for all eternity. Even as you think you are restricted now to your body, know that you are without restriction. In reality, you are free within me. When you take up your true nature, you realise this truth. By taking up your true nature, you know yourself, you know me, and you remember.

CHAPTER 20

The Willingness To Receive

My Pleasure

As you give, so do you receive. As you give, you get pleasure, so allow me the pleasure of giving to you. Open your arms wide and receive all that I give.

Many of you deny me the pleasure of giving because you block yourself from receiving. Be open and willing to receive. You are worthy to receive. So many of you think that you need to give in order to receive, but you misinterpret. Do you not see that it is the giver who gets the most pleasure? Those who have more, I give more to because they accept my gifts with gratitude, allowing me the pleasure of giving. That is why the rich get richer, for they delight in receiving, giving me pleasure. When you genuinely give to someone, expecting nothing in return, you receive pleasure.

Do not deny me the joy of giving, for I can only give to those who are willing to receive. You deny me the joy of giving because of your wrong thinking. As you think, so you are. I enjoy giving to those who enjoy receiving. Open your hearts and your minds, my beloved, and give me joy. Joy is the greatest gift you can give me, just as it is the greatest gift you can receive. In the holy book I instructed you through Jesus to ask and you will receive and your joy will be full. I delight in giving, and when I give, if you are joyous, it gives me so much pleasure.

The Joy Of Giving

My giving is unlimited. It is you who has limits as to what you will receive.

Remove your limits. You are worthy. Allow me to give you the desires of your hearts. The cattle on a thousand hills are mine. All creation belongs to me, and I bestow gifts on those who receive with gratitude.

Joy is within you as you give. As I give to you, you again give to others. Your joy flows full by giving and receiving. When you see someone in need, give to that person expecting nothing back except the joy you get from giving. As you give, you shall receive. Gratitude is the magnet that draws the desires of your heart. Let your whole being resonate with gratitude, thus attracting the vibration of your heart's desire. Even when you have all that you desire, keep giving thanks for all that you are. Give thanks for your contentment. As you do, you are always aware of your alignment with me.

This awareness keeps you in the light and stops you from getting caught up in the illusion. For just like a candle burning in the fog, your light is less bright if it is surrounded by the cloud of illusion. As you raise your vibration to a frequency of constant gratitude, you cement our alignment. As you raise your vibrational frequency, you become even more attuned to me, recognising me as your very substance. As you become more spiritually evolved, more is revealed to you.

Ending The Dream

Spiritual concepts that were beyond understanding at one time become easy for you to grasp as you remember their truth. You have access to divine wisdom, knowledge, and power. Your light shines bright in the wilderness, and souls seeking answers are attracted to you. Your presence radiates a calmness that is not common in the chaos of illusion. Your truth is recognised as you render yourself for service. By following your truth, which is one with mine, you are called by your soul into your divine purpose. Heed the call and feel the peace as you avail yourself to spirit without condition. Go where it leads you. Your soul will direct your words and actions. You may not yet know where you are being led, but you know without a doubt that you are going the right way, according to plan. This surety, this faith of yours, is as steadfast as is your purpose within which you are immersed.

You have accommodated me in every fibre of your being. Your voice, hands, feet, heart, and smile all project me because I am within. I am in you and you are in me, extending the light to the darkness. In this way we expose the illusion as the light of truth dawns. When the light is so widespread, reaching every corner of the earth, even those in the shadows will be able to see. By seeing the truth so clearly illuminated in the light, they will leave their shadow behind, ending their dream.

Communion

You are often so busy in your life of illusion that you talk *of* me but you fail to talk *with* me. I understand you even when you are too busy just to *be* with me, but it is when you look inside yourself, specifically to be present with me, that you witness your eternal beingness. It is then the connection to me is experienced and understood. It is the understanding of our alliance *within* that is vital to understanding your *outer* reality. As you become more and more familiar with yourself and your reality, you make sense of our oneness. Time set aside to be with me is sacred time. I incline my ear to you. Your devoted presence opens the gate in your mind to revelation from your soul. Your soul is my essence within your being. It is your divine self, your true self. It is through your soul that I commune with you. It is during our special communion sessions that you experience my presence.

Commune with me before you rise up in the morning, and joyfully anticipate the day ahead. Confide in me before you lay down to sleep at night, and share with me your secrets. Throughout the day, I am always present. Be mindful of my presence. Often these times are the only times when you are totally aware of my infinite grace. Oh that you would consciously be aware of my grace at all times. I love you with a never-ending love.

Rise Up

I see your trials and tribulations. Nothing happens without my witness. If only you would look within for guidance. If only you would know yourself, you could make straight your own path.

Rise up! Rise up! Rise up in your awareness of me, and take me with you in your every moment. Be constantly aware of my love and guidance for you. I know you intimately—your every movement, your every thought. I am your creator and your friend. You who consider that this life is your only existence, behold, do you not know that you are eternal, forever dwelling in my kingdom of glory? This life is but a dream. You fell asleep by your own choosing, but soon you will wake to the celebration of your glorious existence. The time is soon for your awakening. The scales will fall from your eyes, and once again you will be where you belong—forever with me. You dwell in me, infinitely united.

Transformation Through Grace

Above and beyond your ego's will is the divine will for your life. The divine will for your life is the ultimate fulfilment of your soul's purpose. Many of you chose to follow your ego's will as opposed to your divine will. Those who choose this path will feel that something is missing in their lives regardless of what they have achieved or attained. You are missing inner peace that comes from knowing yourself as soul.

You are missing the point to your very existence.

Your ego's will pales in comparison to your divine will. Your ego's will is not great, it is not fulfilling, and it is not real. The purpose of your soul is all important, regardless, if compared to the purpose of others, it seems mundane. It doesn't matter what the purpose of your soul is as long as you are doing it. Soul only asks for your trust. Your soul is beyond time. It sees the whole picture, and it only wants what is in your best interest. Oh that you would live according to your soul rather than your ego. The riches of my kingdom are within; know that the treasure is your very soul. Seek and you will find. Knock and the door will open for you. All confusion gives way to understanding, and all darkness vanishes in the light. Beloved, it is through grace that you are transformed from your darkness into the light. Grace has always been with you, but it is your acceptance of grace that has allowed her to move in your life.

CHAPTER 21

The Way Of Soul

Death

Your journey through life is a spiritual journey. This journey began when you took form and it ends when you leave form. There is no death except that of your illusion. Death is liberation from form, releasing your soul to freedom.

My beloved, your true nature is pure love. Pure love is pure energy. Your energy is the highest form of energy. It contains all knowledge. Your energy has always existed. You cannot be destroyed, although you can change form. Death is just your energy returning home.

Any fear you may have of death is based on ignorance of your true nature. This fear is a senseless fear, rooted in deceit. It is your ego that deceives you this way. I am not a God of deceit but of truth. Look at your fear of death in the light of your soul and watch as it vanishes. It has no truth. It is just part of your dream.

All fears are of the dark. Therefore, aspire to be in the light. When you are of the light, you see fear as a figment of your imagination, which you can now consciously control. Wake up into the light and walk in confidence and strength in the way of your soul.

I am with you wherever you are.

Your Soul Has A Unique Path

As you become true to your nature, you recognise that you have your own distinct course to follow. Your distinct course is one in which you follow your soul's calling. Each soul is perfectly aligned with me. In me all things are made perfect. Just as sure as your solar system is perfect in its design, so too is the intricate maze of pathways of each soul. There are no collisions with other souls as you advance to your purpose. There is no competition in spirit. Each soul has its own path, and each soul has its own calling. No two are identical. There is no competition because there are no polarities of winning and losing. There is only one path to follow. Each of you follows a unique path, as each of you is unique. All of you have your own path to walk, guided by your soul.

When you awaken to oneness, competitiveness is obsolete.

There is no need to compete with others for love or positions. Each of you has your own place in my divine plan. No individual place is better than any other. By following your soul's will for your life, you follow my divine will because my will and your soul's will for your life are one. When following your soul's will, you know that you are always in the right place. You know you are doing what you were born to do. It feels right to you because you are divine; your way is the higher way. Your divine place is undisputed and undeniably yours. There is nobody competing for that position because it has only ever been yours. There is no competition, only unity, each one separate yet together one.

I Will Prod You

Look inward to me, and trust my voice. I will lead you on the straight path. Do not wonder where you are going in life. Just accept that I am leading you. I will not lead you into darkness, for my paths are well lit. At times you may doubt that you are hearing me correctly, but I tell you that if you go off the path, you will feel me prod you. You will feel the prod and know in your spirit that you are out of my will for your life. If you know that you are not following the path of your soul, look within. When you look within, you hear my voice and attune yourself to it, and then you will feel my peace that surpasses all understanding as you walk forward in the light.

Each Soul A Separate Thread In The Tapestry

In the tapestry of souls, you each do your part to complete the picture of the new dawn where all is light. When this tapestry of the journey of souls is complete, you will all be witness to it. It will reflect unconditional love and unity of beliefs; you will all believe the same to be true. With the completion of the tapestry comes the realisation of the consciousness of oneness. This is not a time to be feared but a time in which to rejoice. It is a time of celebration as the old era makes way for the new.

Welcome the new dawn. Welcome the morning of a new age.

Authenticity

Again I urge you not to slumber, make your transition to the light one of utmost importance. End your suffering on earth, and rejoice in the knowledge of your soul.

Complete satisfaction is gained only when you live according to your soul's wisdom. A void is present within you, a feeling that something is not quite right, when you deny your trueness.

Know yourself, and live in authenticity.

Have a grateful heart for all that you are, and live your life in the full knowledge of your being. Many of you spend hours studying this and that; consider studying yourself. Do you put as much time into spiritual communion with me as you do in activities of far less importance? Seek me first, and all other things will fall into place. Know yourself, learn your true nature, that of your soul, and by doing so, you will know me.

Your true nature holds your true power. Authentic power is made available to you as you draw from yourself. You cannot draw from yourself without knowing who you are. Seek to know yourself, thereby knowing me. In me you live, move, breathe, and have your being. In me your being is home. Your true nature is not one of darkness. My spirit is of the light. Your true nature contains mine. It is love, light, and health. It is grace. Your true nature contains my power, for your true nature *is* my power. When you live in authenticity, you are bold in who you are, beyond judgment and beyond criticism. You know who you are; you know your purpose, and nothing can convince you otherwise. You know with certainty from within that you are on the right track.

The Path Of Soul

Once you are on the right track, life becomes easy. You are no longer swimming against the current. Life no longer feels like an obstacle course. Your way clears, and you now accept your only real choice, knowing it as the soul's calling for your life. All other choices fade as you desire your true path. The path of soul becomes more and more familiar as your journey continues. It feels liberating to walk confidently in the way you know is true. It feels liberating to no longer be tempted by ego's choices.

Ego's choices were always a risk you took. There is no risk in choosing the way of soul. It is always the right choice. It is the way, the truth, and the light. It is the way home. When you know your way home, help others, directing them to their souls. It is only by knowing themselves that these souls will wake up to the light. They in turn will lift their vibration, drawing others with them. The illusion ends when every single one of you understands that we are all one. We are all one, united in light as we wake from our dream of separateness. It is because we are all one that it is vital that each soul wakes to the reality of its eternal union within me because when one believes it is separate; its belief denies its union within me.

It Is Your Choice

You come into this life as a soul in a body, and you identified with others, accepting their biases. Your soul within you was waiting, watching, and loving. When you went the wrong way and made the wrong choices, it was felt in the spirit and communicated through grace to your soul. At times your soul allowed you just to go and hopefully to learn from your mistakes, and at times it nudged you, warning you that it was the wrong decision. Ultimately the decisions were made by your ego, your old nature. These choices were based in fear or ignorance.

Following the voice of your soul leads to happiness, completeness, and fulfilling your divine potential. This is my promise to you. Follow your truth. Even though you recognise the dream you are living in, your connection to soul results in experiencing bliss as you await reunion. Knowing me within yourself, you eagerly anticipate our reunion, assured by spirit that it will be your choice whether to return to this earthly realm.

CHAPTER 22

The Alchemy Of Grace

Can You Hear Me

Listen

I Am Truth

One With All

Be My Hands

Your Soul's Song

Can You Hear Me

I am calling you. Listen within to my voice. You are not mistaken; it is my still, small voice that speaks to you. Enter in. Enter in to my kingdom. Within the kingdom of your soul is the guidance you need to pursue your divine path. Be bold in your spiritual work, and look within for directions. Listen to the voice of your soul. Fear and doubt are replaced with trust and faith. You have all the answers available to you; follow the guidance given to you. Seek to know yourself and know me and all else falls into place. Do not fear the uncertainty of the future, for as you walk according to the guidance you receive, your next step will become clear.

All through life you have had many choices, and many times you have agonised over decisions you have had to make. Beloved, choosing to follow your soul means you no longer struggle with choice, having faith that you are being led in the best way for you. At first you may question the direction because it may not seem to make sense to you, but learn to trust. The way you are headed and the situations you find yourself in are perfect.

Your soul is the eternal you. It cannot lead you astray. Your soul knows all your limitations and all your strengths. Your soul is one with me. There is no difference between your soul's voice and my voice. We are one, and in that way I speak to you through soul, listen.

Listen

Listen to me within your soul. Do not be mistaken—the voice of love you hear is mine. You are my beloved. I dwell within you, and you dwell within me. Turn inward and acknowledge me. Trust in my voice, and believe the truths I share with you. It is only by following the voice of your soul that you will walk your true path. No longer faced with making difficult decisions, you do what feels right in your soul, confident as you accept the right way for your life. It clearly becomes the only way. When you walk in my truths, reflecting the light of my presence within you, you are more sensitive to the needs of others, and the love within you reaches out to them.

The light and the love reflected through your eyes to others is often all that is needed to kindle the search for truth within themselves. Your light shines through their darkness, replacing their fear of the unknown with hope and optimism of a new way for them. As your light touches their souls, it then becomes illuminated, and for many this is their first glimpse of what lies within them. It is only by knowing what is within them that they can really know what lies beyond. Within each of you lies your soul. By knowing your soul, you know me because your soul is your true nature within which I dwell. I do not abide in ego because it is not true.

I Am Truth

I am truth; your soul is truth. It is truth that sets you free. There is no darkness in the light. I am not promising that you will not have any sadness in your life, but I am promising that you will see things from a different perspective, and knowing yourself, you draw on your authentic strength and wisdom. You, who have felt alone in your sorrowing times, know that you were never alone. You were never alone then, and you are never alone now. When things in your life bring you pain, and when life doesn't appear to make sense, look inside and listen to the great comforter. The peace you find within your soul counteracts any distress. Just as the passing of time on your planet seems to lessen grief, in eternity, timeless reality, grief cannot exist.

My love for you is so strong. I care about your every need. You are my precious creation, my masterpiece, and in you I dwell. Oh turn from your despair over past events and look to me. Look for me. You find me within your soul. I am one with your soul. I am the light in your darkness, I am love, and I am everywhere.

I *am* calling your name. I wait on you to answer.

One With All

There are those who now believe in the truth of oneness, but I say unto you that unless you can see your soul reflected in the eyes of every single person on this earth, then you have not completely understood. My beloved, being one with me is not about what is in it for you. It is not about having a connection or about having abundant life, although these are a small part of it. The truth of oneness is love in motion; it is seeing and treating others as yourself.

There are no exclusions: the drunk, the prostitute, every race, every religion, every orphan, and every king, they are all one with you. Jesus taught compassion, not exclusion. He taught giving from the heart to all the needy, not just giving to those in your little group who obey the same laws as you. But now in your awareness, send out love and light to all of mankind. It is divine love that connects you to all living things. You are in it, and it is in you. My love is in all of you, but some of you are more aware of it than others.

I am a God of compassion and grace. You are one with me. Be true to your divine nature, and live your life in the spirit of oneness the way it is intended to be lived. You are all equal, and you are all one. You are all my precious children. Each one of you is connected through love to every other person. You are all one. As you grow in your spirituality, you pass the toddler stage where it was all about you and your walk with me. Now as you mature, you reach out to encompass all of mankind in oneness.

Be My Hands

Many of you are coming into maturity now and are able to see that others living in poverty and disease are an extension of yourself. It is through *you* that balance, equality, and oneness spread over the earth and darkness and suffering end. Darkness and suffering are a result of wrong thinking. Your righteous thinking is the light of love that shines on every single man, woman, and child. No starving child and no homeless tramp can escape your love. Be my hands, be my feet, be my voice, and be my heart to all. Be my love working through you to unite all people in grace. Divine oneness is in you, and you are in it. Nobody is excluded, and all are equal.

Do not become obsessed with the injustices of the world. Know they are part of the dream, but do not become indifferent either.

You can have compassion for those who are suffering without internalising their grief. Knowing the problems that occur in the world, walk in the way your soul will have you go, and trust that soul will call on you to help in the appropriate way.

Faith without works is dead. Help may not always be in the physical, but give of your spirit. Send light and love by mode of conscious thought to those in need. Listen to your soul and you will be guided. The energy you direct your thoughts with will bring relief in some form to those who are struggling. Be my hands, be my feet, be my voice, and be my heart. Extend your love out to all.

Your Soul's Song

Feel love in your soul, know yourself as love, and reach out to others as you put your love in action. As you join together in the spirit of oneness, you impact the world, drawing others into the light, strong in your vision and putting your faith into action. Mankind joins together each precious person a part of the whole. Act on your faith, share your truth both practically and spiritually, and do not stop until you have reached out to every single person. Even one small act of kindness makes a difference and is better than indifference. Live your oneness by grace, and transform this world.

My beloved, choosing to live a life with all your goals defined by your ego mind is so vastly different than living your life according to your soul.

You each have etched in your soul a sacred path to follow, and as you follow your soul, you are aware of a great peace.

The longing, the searching, and the feeling of incompleteness are gone; you are home. You are reconciled with your true nature—no more wandering in the wilderness, no more doubt.

Knowing yourself, you know me, and you are complete in me. Your life now feels so comfortable, so natural, and so right. Each day is appreciated afresh as you sing your soul's song—a song of happiness, gratitude, and love—*a song testifying to your transformation through the alchemy of grace.*

The End

My Words

These are my words. You may be called to write such words, but these words are birthed in me. Many will bear inner witness to their truth, for I am truth. In truth you may write according to your inner witness.

I say unto you what has been revealed to you through spirit is but the tip of the iceberg. Humble yourself to my presence, be a clear channel and a messenger of light. I will speak through you if you will just make my way clear. All mankind will proclaim my grace. My grace honours the individual soul yet encompasses the all, and my grace abounds forever.